word

Finding our place in God's creation

The Healing
Word

Bishop Basil of Amphipolis

Edited by Jessica Rose

DARTON · LONGMAN + TODD

First published in 2008 by
Darton, Longman and Todd Ltd
1 Spencer Court
140 – 142 Wandsworth High Street
London SW18 4JJ

ISBN 0–232–52737–7
ISBN 978–0–232–52737–7

A catalogue record for this book is available from the British
Library.

Designed and produced by Sandie Boccacci
Set in 11/12.75pt Apollo
Printed and bound in Great Britain by
CPI Antony Rowe, Chippenham

Contents

Foreword

Eastern Orthodox Christians have regularly reminded their brothers and sisters in the West that the good news of Jesus Christ is not primarily a message of reassurance to isolated individuals; it is the restoration of an entire environment. To be taken into the Body of Christ is to be made at one with God and with God's creation. Just as in the ritual of the Temple in ancient Israel, so now the whole world is symbolically evoked and its reconciliation displayed when the Church of Christ gathers for worship.

Bishop Basil spells out in this brief but profound and authoritative study how healing promised by the gospel reaches to every area of our identity as material creatures. To be redeemed is to be absolved and liberated, certainly, but it is also to be given once again the place in creation for which humans were created. And once we speak of a place for which we were created, we are also committed to thinking about the pattern of the created universe as a harmony of seen and unseen levels of energy. Perhaps the most original feature of this book is that it uses the Christian philosophy of the Church Fathers to suggest how we might today begin a fruitful intellectual engagement with the world of contemporary physics and cosmology. Ancient treatises on the orders of angels turn out to be full of insights that help us make sense of the interlocking and interweaving fields of force and levels of organisation that are uncovered by contemporary science. And to understand the universe in this way saves us from various kinds of reductionism and allows us to take completely seriously every aspect of our concrete sense experience.

The reader may be surprised to find a deeply traditional Christian theology offering so robust a perspective on the significance of the body and the environment, and providing such resourceful tools for a positive appreciation of the scientific world view. But such surprise is a sad measure of how our expectations of theology have become far too low. Bishop Basil demonstrates how, if we bring higher expectations to our Christian thinking, we end up also with the highest expectations of redeemed humanity – and thus the highest possible appreciation of the scope and scale of Christ's redeeming work and God's creative purpose. It is wonderful to have a book like this from a learned, imaginative and prayerful mind, a book which so enlarges our horizons and intensifies our gratitude and delight in the new creation.

+ Rowan Cantuar:
Lambeth Palace, London
Pentecost 2008

Healing in the Life of the Individual

1

The Healing Power of God's Word

When Peter stood up to preach on Pentecost there was no 'New Testament'. There were no 'Christian' scriptures to which he could refer. Much of what he said was simply comment on the scriptures that he did know, and which he understood in the light of something else he knew: that Jesus of Nazareth was the Messiah, the Christ, whom God had raised from the dead. It was the story of this man, and Peter's own experience as one of his disciples, that enabled him to understand the familiar scriptures in a new way and at greater depth than ever before. In other words, he was reading into the scriptures his own experience.

Since Peter's time, little has changed. Preaching the 'word' is still largely the result of finding in the scriptures what we already know – and there are good reasons why this should be so. No text explains itself completely, even if it is a set of mathematical formulae.

We bring something to what we find there.

The origins of this book lie in the experience of the Eucharist – the Divine Liturgy – but it is based not so much on the *words* that are used during the Liturgy, as on the experience of corporate, liturgical prayer, and the sense of oneness that comes through sacramental communion. This oneness takes several forms. It can be oneness with the others who are sharing in the prayer. It can be oneness with Christ and the Father in the Spirit. It can be oneness with 'those who have gone to their rest before us, and who here, and in all the world, lie asleep in the Lord'. It can even be an inner oneness with ourselves, an integration of our being at all levels that is greater than what we experience in everyday life.

All aspects of this feeling of oneness bring with them a sense of healing, a sense that the scatteredness of life has been overcome and that we have found our proper place in God's world. Reconciliation has taken place. Atonement – at-*one*-ment – has been realised not through our own personal efforts, but by plunging ourselves deep into the givenness of the life of the Church.

The reflections that follow are an attempt to look at some of the areas that concern all Christians today. It will take the form of a journey, tracing the healing power of God's Word in personal experience, in the life of the Church, and finally in the cosmic role of the Church as the continuing incarnation of Christ. We will find ourselves drawing on three major sources: scripture itself, the liturgical texts of the Orthodox Church, and finally the profound, intuitive appreciations of the created world that have been bequeathed us by the early Church Fathers.

Because we suffer today as a culture from a strange inability to link our present with our past, this journey will involve bringing together the experience of Jesus

Christ that we find in the Gospels with contemporary insights into human behaviour, with the cosmology of the Fathers, especially Dionysius the Areopagite and Maximus the Confessor, and with the contemporary 'scientific' view of the world. These Fathers were not scientists in the modern sense, nor indeed were they even philosophers, but they were in touch with creation at depth, and were able to speak of it from an existential stance that still has much to offer today.

All faiths, all religions, try to grasp the whole to the extent that this is possible for human beings. After all, the word 'religion' itself comes from a Latin root meaning 'to bind together'. One of the insights of the Fathers – and it is not theirs alone – is that the large can be found in the small and, conversely, that the small can be found in the large. The universe is ultimately a single integrated whole – and in God each part of it is linked with every other.

Our challenge today is to find a point from which we can look upon the world as a whole and grasp its true meaning. For the Christian this means, in the end, acquiring, to whatever extent we can, 'the mind of Christ': the healing Word who unites everything in himself – from the minutiae of our day to day experience to the deep structure of everything that exists.

2

Experience of God: the Emerging Word

It is one thing, like Peter, to have experienced a relationship with Jesus – but can we have experience of God? This is a very difficult question, yet there are many accounts of experience of God in the tradition of the Church and in the Bible – both the Old Testament and the New – and then we have the Eucharist. All these form one continuous development, in which we eventually find that such experience applies to each one of us personally. God reveals himself, he talks to us, and finally he becomes visible – living among us as a human being. As the culmination of this process, through the Eucharist, he creates the Church, in which we all participate in the life of God through communion.

The Old Testament: a God who takes the initiative
Throughout the scriptures we encounter human beings who are able to hear God speaking to them. What we

find is that God is a self-revealing God. He does not wait for us to discover him: the initiative is his. Even in the Garden of Eden, he does not wait for Adam to speak: right from the start he instructs Adam as to what he is to do – and also tells him what he is not to do:

> The Lord God took the man, and put him into the garden of Eden to till it and to keep it. And the Lord God commanded the man, saying, 'You may freely eat of every tree of the garden; but of the tree of the knowledge of good and evil, you shall not eat, for in the day that you eat of it, you shall die' (Gen 2:15).

God is the God who acts, who speaks, and who commands. Yet after the commandment has been disobeyed, after the Fall, he does not cease to communicate. Rather, we find an enquiring God. When Adam and Eve have hidden themselves amongst the trees of the garden, he calls out, 'Where are you?' (Gen 3:9).

Then, later on in Genesis, we find a God who not only commands human beings, but makes promises. When he calls Abraham into a special relationship with him, he promises him he will receive his blessing and become a great nation: 'and in you all the families of the earth shall be blessed' (Gen 12:3). God has the future in mind. Further on in this same story we find a God who also makes covenants, when he appears to Abraham and tells him – even at the advanced age of ninety-nine – that he will be 'the father of a multitude of nations'. 'I will establish my covenant between me and you,' says God, 'and your offspring after you throughout their generations, for an everlasting covenant (Gen 17:7). The God who creates and commands is also the God who makes covenants with his creatures.

There are countless episodes in the Old Testament

where God reveals himself as a God who speaks to human beings. Sometimes, as in Genesis 18, in the scene depicted by Andrei Rublev in his famous fourteenth-century icon of the Old Testament Trinity, God does not speak directly, but communicates through angels. Three angels appear to Abraham in the plain of Mamre, and it is through them that the Lord appears to him. Similarly, in Genesis 19, two angels come to Lot at Sodom. Much more common, however, is the direct address, for example in Genesis 22, in the story of the sacrifice of Isaac:

> After these things, God tested Abraham. He said to him, 'Abraham!' And he said, 'Here I am'. He said, 'Take your son, your only son Isaac, whom you love, and go to the land of Moriah; and offer him there as a burnt offering on one of the mountains that I shall show you' (Gen 22:1–2).

The impact of these words on Abraham can hardly be imagined. God seems to be going back on his promise to make him the 'father of a multitude of nations'. With the death of Isaac his line will die out. In the end, of course, God speaks again to Abraham and tells him not to lay his hand on the boy, but to sacrifice the ram caught in the thicket near him instead.

Probably the most dramatic example of God speaking, however, is to be found in the story of Moses, in the incident of the burning bush, which took place while Moses was tending the flock of Jethro, his father-in-law. As he led the flock through the desert, he came across a bush that was on fire but was not consumed by the flames. Moses turned aside to take a closer look, and 'when the Lord saw that he turned aside to see, God called to him out of the bush, "Moses, Moses!" and he said, "Here I am"' (Ex 3:4). The voice of God is recognisable, even when he simply calls Moses by name, and from then on he continues to guide Moses as to what to do, to deal with his anxieties and lack of confidence, and to show him how to bring his people out of Egypt. Chapters 6 through 14 of Exodus all begin with the words 'The Lord said to Moses ...'.

It is on Mount Sinai, however, that Moses truly becomes the first of the prophets – the first of those who hear the word of God and pass it on to the people. God calls to Moses out of the mountain and says: 'Thus you shall say to the house of Jacob, and tell the Israelites: You have seen what I did to the Egyptians, and how I bore you on eagles' wings, and brought you to myself. ... These are the words that you shall speak to the Israelites' (Ex 19:3). Moses calls the elders of the people and conveys to them everything that the Lord tells him. He is not only the recipient of God's word: he is also a mediator between God and human beings.

In the story of the prophet Samuel a very interesting point emerges. Samuel was born to his mother Hannah against all expectations and as a result she offered him to the Lord. The boy then served the priest Eli, whose eyesight was growing dim so that he could not see. Samuel was sleeping in the temple where the ark of the covenant was kept, and heard God call his name. He thought it was Eli calling to him and ran to serve him. Eli, of course, told him that he had not called for him and Samuel went back to his place and slept. The same thing happened a second time. No, Eli had not called for him. Finally, the third time, Eli realised that it was the Lord who was calling the boy, and told him to go back and, if he heard the same voice, to say, 'Speak, Lord, for your servant is listening' (1 Sam 3:10). Samuel did this, and from that time on the Lord spoke frequently to him. We are dealing, then, with a God who not only speaks, but is willing to repeat himself if he does not get through the first time. This pattern occurs again and again with the other prophets.

With Isaiah, however, we find a further complexity in the gift of prophecy. Speech is combined with vision in a strange, paradoxical encounter that seems to describe a combination of seeing and hearing:

> The vision of Isaiah, the son of Amoz, which he saw concerning Judah and Jerusalem in the days of Uzziah, Jotham, Ahaz and Hezekiah, kings of Judah. 'Hear, O heavens, and listen, O earth: for the Lord hath spoken' (Isa 1:1).

We already know that God speaks to creation, just as he does in the very beginning: 'God said, "Let there be light", and there was light' (Gen 1:3). His word is an active and creative word. Yet it is not just that God speaks and the world is called into being: the world itself speaks:

> The heavens are telling the glory of God; and the firmament proclaims his handiwork. Day to day pours forth speech, and night to night declares knowledge. There is no speech, nor are there words; their voice is not heard; yet their voice goes out through all the earth, and their words to the end of the world (Ps 19:1–4).

We perceive something in the beauty, complexity and grandeur of creation that is not just what we see with our eyes, nor what we understand intuitively of God, but a 'word' that expresses the relationship between these two, between creation and the Creator. In this sense we can say that creation does not just speak *about* God. It is in some sense the voice of God addressing us, through which he speaks to us about himself. In this it can be likened to a poet's experience of God in nature.

Another way in which God speaks in the Old Testament is through miracles. It is through a series of miracles – the plagues on Egypt, the Passover, the parting of the Red Sea in Exodus 14 – that the Jewish people are brought out of Egypt and experience salvation, something which has marked the consciousness not only of the Jewish people, but that of Christians ever since. God reveals himself as saviour not only to individuals, but in the historical experience of a people. Thus salvation becomes in some sense an event outside time, one that lives in the memory, which is always present, and is reflected in the worshipping experience of a people.

The New Testament: a God who can be seen as well as heard

The New Testament writings reflect an experience of God that is different in many ways from what we find in the older scriptures. In the Gospels Christ offers himself to his disciples as a God who can be perceived, not in a vision or through a bodiless voice, but with the physical, bodily senses. We continue to find a God who speaks, of course, but the 'word' is more clearly and openly expressed.

In the Gospel of John we see again and again how John, as he gets behind the image of Christ presented in the synoptic Gospels, brings out new aspects of the 'word' of God. For example, quite early in his Gospel Jesus says, 'It is the spirit that gives life, the flesh is useless. The words that I have spoken to you are spirit and life' (Jn 6:63). The words of God carry with them the spirit, the breath of God as well, fanning and causing to burst out into flame the embers that lie in the heart of every human being. Just after this, Jesus confronts the fact that some of his disciples are turning away from him, and he asks the twelve, 'Do you also wish to go away?' Simon Peter answers for the rest, 'Lord, to whom can we go? You have the words of eternal life' (Jn 6:66). The 'word' of God in Christ brings with it the Spirit of God, and with the Spirit comes divine life.

The words of Jesus are words of eternal life, and when received inwardly they convey that life. As John makes clear, however, they are not simply Jesus' own words. In his prayer to the Father during the Last Supper, Christ says, '... the words that you gave to me I have given to [my disciples], and they have received them and know in truth that I came from you; and they have believed that you sent me' (Jn 17:8). He goes on to pray, 'Sanctify them in the truth; your word is truth' (Jn 17:17). Earlier on, in John 14, Jesus had already said: 'The words that I say to you I do not speak on my own; but the Father who dwells in me does his works (Jn 14:10). The 'words' of Christ are the 'works' of the Father.

Like Moses, Jesus acts as a mediator of the word of God to his followers. It is the same God who speaks in the Old Testament, but in the New Testament this prophetic word is expanded and extended in two directions.

In the first place, it is extended upwards and backwards. This is made clear, of course, in the opening sentences of the Gospel of John, where the 'word' of God becomes the 'Word' of God:

> In the beginning was the Word, and the Word was with God, and the Word was God. He was in the beginning with God; all things came into being through him; and without him not one thing came into being. What has come into being in him was life; and the life was the light of all people (Jn 1:1–4).

The Word of God, which became flesh and was revealed in Christ, has been 'with' God from the beginning, from before the creation of the world. The Word of God in Christ is other than the Father, and yet is identified with the creative power of God that is reflected in creation. To use the language of St Paul, Christ is 'the power of God, and the wisdom of God' (1 Cor 1:23), and the power and wisdom of God are eternal. The meaning of the word 'Word' and its expression in Christ is extended upwards into the divine and taken back to the beginning, to the moment of creation and beyond.

At another level, however, the activity of that same Word is now extended downwards into the material world, and forwards towards us. The opening passage of the Gospel of John expresses this as well when it says: 'The Word became flesh and lived among us' (Jn 1:14). In the earlier scriptures, as we have seen, the heavens speak: they are capable of mediating the Word of God to human beings. But in John, the Word of God speaks through the incarnate Christ, the Word become flesh. Indeed, it no longer speaks *through* the material world, but has become *one* with Jesus, who is himself embodied in the material world. This is something new. In what can now legitimately be called the 'incarnation' of the Word of God, 'we have seen his glory, the glory as of a father's only son, full of grace and truth' (Jn 1:14). In the incarnate Word, the glory of God the Father is made visible not only to the eyes of the soul, but to the eyes of the body.

This is taken even further in the First Epistle of John:

> We declare to you what was from the beginning, what we have heard, what we have seen with our eyes, what we have looked at and touched with our hands, concerning the word of life – the life was revealed, and we have seen it and testify to it, and

> declare to you the eternal life that was with the
> Father and was revealed to us … (1 Jn 1:1–2).

This is quite extraordinary language. The author refers
to a Word of God that 'was from the beginning', which
was 'with God', which is the 'word of life', 'eternal life'
– and yet he can also speak of it as being something he
has looked at, which his eyes have seen, which his hands
have touched, and whose voice he has heard with his
own ears.

The institution of the Eucharist creates the Church

What is also extraordinary, however, in terms of the
development of Christianity and its eventual break with
Judaism, is the institution of the Eucharist. The account
in Matthew uses language that is so concrete that it
approaches that of the Epistle of John:

> While they were eating, Jesus took a loaf of bread,
> and after blessing it, he broke it, gave it to the dis-
> ciples and said, 'Take, eat; this is my body.' Then
> he took a cup, and after giving thanks, he gave it to
> them, saying, 'Drink of it, all of you, for this is my
> blood of the covenant which is poured out for
> many for the forgiveness of sins' (Mt 26: 26–29).

A similarly striking concreteness is found elsewhere in
the language of Jesus, as reported by John:

> Jesus then said to them, 'I am the bread of life.
> Whoever comes to me will never be hungry, and
> whoever believes in me shall never be thirsty …
> Your ancestors ate manna in the wilderness, and
> they died. This is the bread that comes down from
> heaven, so that one may eat of it, and not die. I am
> the living bread that came down from heaven.
> Whoever eats of this bread will live for ever; and

the bread that I will give for the life of the world is my flesh.' The Jews then disputed among themselves, saying, 'How can this man give us his flesh to eat?' (Jn 6:35, 49–52).

The people listening to Christ interpret his language in a very concrete way: they think he is speaking of his actual flesh. We might even want to say that the break with Judaism is already complete at that point. The Mosaic Laws of purity and impurity forbid anyone to eat meat with the blood still in it. It is absolutely forbidden, and it is inconceivable that pious Jews would do such a thing. Even less could they contemplate eating human flesh with its blood. Yet for St Paul, writing not so many years after the Crucifixion, participation in the body and blood of Christ through the Eucharist is the foundation of the oneness of the Church both with itself and ultimately with Christ:

> I speak as to sensible people; judge for yourselves what I say. The cup of blessing that we bless, is it not a sharing in the blood of Christ? The bread that we break, is it not a sharing in the body of Christ? Because there is one bread, we who are many are one body, for we all partake of the one bread (1 Cor 10:15–17).

We see here in St Paul's thought the way the bread and the cup create the Church, yet in doing this he simply carries on and develops the words Christ spoke to the Jews in the Gospel of John. There Christ is talking about communion with himself, but for Paul, the reality of eucharistic worship, with its breaking of the loaf in order that all may eat, leads him to think of the oneness of the original loaf, and then of the oneness of Christ in whom all participate through eating their portion of the one bread. Finally he concludes that we are all one, we are the Body of Christ, because we share in a single loaf. The Eucharist creates the Church in the sense that communion in the one bread and the one cup unites the members of the Church to Christ and to one another. This is the central mystery of the New Testament, the mystery of our participation in the life of God through the sacrament of communion in the Body and Blood of Christ.

This very brief overview shows that we are dealing with an extraordinary continuity, a gradually developing relationship between the God who speaks and creates, the God who speaks and addresses human beings, and the God whose people hear him and respond. If we go back to the beginning and ask ourselves how Adam knew that his name was Adam, we can only assume that God told him so by calling him by his name. How else could he know what he was called, unless when he heard the word 'Adam' he understood intuitively that this was the mediating 'word' that linked him with his Creator. In this case his response might well have been a wordless 'Here I am', anticipating the responses of Abraham, Moses and the prophet Samuel. In any case, the conversation begins with God – indeed, with the Word of God – speaking first.

A dialogue began then that continues to this day, for God continues to reveal himself through creation, through the scriptures, through his conversation with individual human beings. And in case we have somehow failed to hear our own name, in Revelation 2:17 we are told that in the end we shall all be given a small white stone on which our name is written, a name known to no one else and which is our own personal link with the Father in Christ.

3

Meeting Jesus Christ

We have been speaking of what it means to 'hear' Christ' and to 'see' him. This is just the first stage in the process, however, whereby we draw near to God. We need to 'meet' Christ as well.

Truly to meet Jesus — as to meet truly any human being — means to be with him where he is. This is the point of a number of sayings of Jesus found in the Gospel of John in which Christ uses the expression, 'where I am'. These are, in a way, a subclass of the great 'I am' sayings in which he sets out his relationship to the Father, but these particular sayings focus primarily on our being with Christ — and therefore with the Father.

The first of these passages occurs in a conflict situation, when the people are beginning to 'murmur' and say that the miracles they see may be evidence that Jesus is in fact the Christ, the Anointed One of God. As a result, the Pharisees send officers to arrest him. Jesus says to the officers, 'I will be with you a little while longer, and then I am going to him who sent me. You will search for me, but you will not find me: and where I am, you cannot come' (Jn 7:33). These words understandably puzzle his hearers. Indeed, Jesus seems to be deliberately provoking his audience, even though he knows them to be hostile. In the end, he leaves the question open, and does not tell them where he will go, or where he will be.

Later in John's account, when Jesus has gone up to Jerusalem to celebrate the Jewish Passover with his people for the last time, John describes him as saying: 'Very truly, I tell you, unless a grain of wheat falls into the earth and dies, it remains just a single grain [abides alone.'[1] This word, 'abide' (*menei*), is usually used in John to refer to close personal contact and presence, but here its use serves to give emphasis to the notion of distance, of separation: no one would wish to *abide* alone. 'But if it dies,' Jesus continues, 'it bears much fruit. Those who love their life lose it; and those who hate their life in this world will keep it for eternal life' (Jn 12:24ff.).

What comes through in this passage is the contrast between a self-centred survival and the sacrificial death that leads to eternal life. What is more, this sacrificial death is linked to following Christ, to serving him. This is the gateway to being with Christ *where he is*: 'If any one serves me, he must follow me; and *where I am*, there shall my servant be also.' The point is taken up again in a poetic parallelism that tells us that to be with Christ, to be where he is, is a gift of the Father: 'If any one serves me, the Father will honour him' (Jn 12:26). In this passage we have learned what it takes to be with Christ, but we have not yet learned where he is.

In John 14 Jesus again makes use of the expression 'where I am'. He has just told Peter that Peter will deny him three times, and as if to raise the disciples' spirits after this, he then goes on to say, 'Do not let your hearts be troubled: believe in God [i.e. the Father], believe also in me. In my Father's house are many dwelling-places.' This word 'dwelling-places' (*monai*) is important here, since for any speaker of Greek it will at once be associated with *menein*, 'to abide'. 'Dwelling-places' are where one 'abides'. 'If it were not so,' he goes on, 'would I have told you that I go to prepare a place for you? And if I go and prepare a place for you, I will come again and will take you to myself, so that where I am, there you may be also' (Jn 14:1–3).

At this point Christ once again faces incomprehension. When he says immediately afterward, 'You know the way to the place where I am going,' Thomas says to him: 'Lord, we do not know not where you are going. How can we know the way?' It turns out, of course, in the next verse, that Jesus himself is 'the way', and that 'no one comes to the Father, except through me' (Jn 14:6). What is interesting here, however, is that we now know that to be with Christ is to be with the Father.

The final passage in this series is from Christ's high priestly prayer in John 17. Christ has been talking of his oneness with the Father and his longing that his followers should be one with him and thus one with his Father. He goes on to say: 'Father, I desire that those also, whom you have given me, be with me where I am; to see my glory, which you have given me because you loved me before the foundation of the world' (Jn 17:24). Here we learn that to be where Christ is – and thus to be where the Father is as well – is to be in a position to behold his glory. This is surely an important indication as to where *we* must be in order to be with Christ, and therefore in the deepest sense *meet* him. We can assume that this is where we want to be, but at the same time we need to ask ourselves how we will react to his presence. There are several indications of this in the Gospels.

What happens when we meet Christ?

One story that is told in all three synoptic Gospels – Matthew, Mark and Luke – is known as the story of the Gadarene swine – though the swine are by no means the most important element in the narrative. What is important is the relationship between the demonic powers and Christ.

Christ is met by two men 'possessed with devils'. What does this actually mean for us in this twenty-first century? In the most general sense, it means that the image of God in them has been seriously obscured. The reason for this, as we shall see later, is that the inner person has become aligned with the fallen angels, the 'demons', and that the outer person has become a reflection of that inner reality. In the case of the two men in this story, this is true to such an extent that it appears as if the demons themselves are speaking through these individuals. What is striking, therefore, is that the demons recognise Christ, even though they do not seem to have to been told about him. This is not the only time in the Gospels that something like this happens. There are other incidents, also, when the demonic powers are actually more aware of what is going on than the Apostles themselves. This can only mean that these hidden, fallen powers are actually closely in touch with the fundamental unseen reality of this world, with its deepest Truth. They refuse to accept it, however. They refuse to live in accordance with it.

The demons ask Christ, 'What have you to do with us, Son of God? Have you come here to torment us before the time?'(Mt 8:29). Not only do the demons recognise that Jesus is the Son of God; they also recognise that he is opposed to them, that he is here to torment them, to make their life difficult. He is, in fact, their adversary. But even more interesting, it seems to me, is that they know that their present confrontation with Christ is not definitive. They expect the true confrontation to take place at some future – but appointed – time. If Christ were to respond to their question, he would have had to have said, 'Yes, I *have* come to torment you before the time, before the *end* of time and the consummation of all things.' In some strange way they already know what their fate is, just as we, the readers of the Gospel, are expected to know what it is. The demons themselves, in other words, are aware of God's plan for salvation. They are in touch with the whole thrust of God's will for mankind. But we, too, as creatures of God, are guided by hidden powers. We know, simply by virtue of our createdness and our contact with our own inner nature – intuitively and instinctively – the pull of God's will for us, but we do not allow ourselves to be guided by God's will.

At the same time we, too, like the demons, recognise Christ and connect him with our future and what we are called to be. Thus we, too, experience him as a challenge and in some sense as an adversary of our fallen state. In the Gospel story, the demons react by seeking to step aside and avoid confrontation. They say to themselves, in effect, 'We had better slip away and do our work elsewhere' – in this case, in the swine, and Christ lets them do this. He says, 'Go!', and they do just that. The men are cured when their demons depart, but other things begin to go seriously wrong. The swine rush down the hill and are drowned.

The inhabitants of the nearby village behave in much the same way as the demons. When they hear what has happened, they come out and confront Jesus and ask him to leave. They do not want to receive Christ. They do not want to confront Christ as he is, with the power he has to heal. They may not know as much about their relationship with Christ as the demons do, but they do know that they do not want to meet him. This applies to all societies, including our own. All societies are in some fundamental way fallen and based on a distortion of the truth. They do not want to face up to Christ, and to bring his understanding of what it means to be human into their understanding of social life. The result is that we as individuals cannot – and should not – expect much support from society as we struggle to be followers of Christ. It is easy to think that all is well when the 'powers that be' approve of us, but the 'powers that be' – and we have to confront this – are also fallen, and have their own relationship with the hidden rulers of the darkness of this world.

Assenting to healing

Our own healing can only come about if we ourselves desire it. In the story of the man lying by the pool of Bethesda in John 5, Jesus goes up to him and asks: 'Do you want to be well?'

This is in fact a very difficult question to answer truthfully. An indication of this in the story is the way in which the paralysed man does not reply directly. Rather, he begins by explaining *why* it is that he has not been healed: he cannot get down into the water fast enough when the water is troubled by the angel, because he has no one to help him. From this answer, however, it is not entirely clear that he really *does* want to be healed. His reply could easily be an excuse. Nevertheless Jesus, perhaps hearing something in his tone of voice, some urgency in the way he speaks, takes his reply to mean 'yes', and tells him to stand up, to take up the mat on which he is lying, and go his way.

This particular passage from the Gospel is read each year during Eastertide. The reason is obvious: it is because this standing up, this 'rising' that Christ enables the man by the pool to perform, is an image of the Resurrection, an image of *our* resurrection at the last day. It is also an image of what can take place in our own lives *now*, before the end. Like the man who lay there paralysed for so many years, we too can get up and walk. We too can be made whole. We too can be healed. This is not, however, likely to happen unless we want it to take place. One of the questions Christ is asking us again and again, whether we are aware of it or not, is just this: 'Do you want to be made whole?' 'Do you want to experience the changes that will be required if you are to live your life in a way that is closer to the promise God sees in you?' It is a searching question, and penetrates to the very heart of our being.

In most of us – perhaps in all of us, to some extent – there is something that resists rebirth, something that resists resurrection, something that resists our being made whole. We are used to the way we are. We do not really *want* to change; or perhaps we do not really believe that any significant change can ever take place – in our feelings about ourselves, in our relationship with others, or in our relationship with God.

In the Book of Revelation Christ says: 'Listen! I am standing at the door, knocking; if you hear my voice, and open the door, I will come in …' (Rev 3:20). What kind of knock does Christ give when he stands at the door? Is it a knock that demands entrance? That would be completely out of character. Christ does not force himself on us. It is simply a knock, and therefore we have to be prepared to hear that knock, even if there are other things going on that attract our attention. Implicit in that knock, that gentle but persistent summons to awake from sleep and let Christ in, is the question: 'Do you wish to be made whole?' 'Do you wish to overcome whatever needs to be overcome in your life?' Positive assent to Christ is necessary if we are to experience his healing.

In all this there is a great freedom, a freedom given to us by God and never taken away. We are in position to invite God into our world through our relationship with Christ. We can prolong the presence of Christ in the world in our hearts, in the temple of our bodies, for Christ lives within us to the extent that we live in him. We are in a position to change. As St Paul said: 'If any-one is in Christ, there is a new creation: everything old has passed away; see, everything has become new!' (2 Cor 5:17).

The conflict inherent in imitation

We could ask ourselves, then, should we relate to Christ by imitating him – and if so, how should we imitate him? Imitation is one of the most common ways we have of relating to anyone. We seem to be destined to this from birth, as it is so clearly the way that infants learn. We even encourage this, almost instinctively, by provid-ing gestures and sounds for them to copy. Imitation is often a form of hidden flattery, and we do feel strangely flattered when a little child deigns to imitate us. What are we risking if we try to imitate the Son of God?

In Matthew 9 we find the story of two miracles of healing performed by Jesus: the healing of the two blind men, and then of the man afflicted by a 'dumb spirit', someone who could not speak. The second of these heal-ings is too much for the Pharisees, who have been watching what is going on. They say, with indignation, 'By the ruler of demons [this man] casts out the demons' (Mt 9:34).

Two things are significant here. The first is that the Pharisees accept that the healings have taken place. They are real. The second is that in their eyes, Jesus, while appearing to do good, is in fact an agent of Satan. It is through Satan, the prince of demons, that he works his miracles. They are not alone, of course, in thinking that what appears to be good can come from the enemy of God. In 2 Corinthians St Paul himself says that 'even Satan disguises himself as an angel of light' (2 Cor 11:14). This is something that we all have to learn: that things are not always what they seem. This presents us with difficulties, both as regards other people, and, even more importantly, as regards ourselves. If things are not what they seem, how can we tell what is really going on within us or in front of us? How, when it is necessary, can we unmask Satan?

Now Satan, by definition, is 'the opponent', the adversary of God, but he is also an *imitator* of God and of the godly forces of good, as both St Paul and the Pharisees realise. It is this aspect of imitation that is one of the most important clues to unmasking Satan, because imitation is – or easily can be – a hidden form of rivalry. To imitate someone is not just flattery. It is also a way of setting oneself up 'over against' another. To imitate someone is to say, in effect, 'I want to be like you,' and it takes only one small step for this to become: 'I want to be where you are.' 'I want to occupy the space, the position that you occupy.' From there it is another small step to: 'What you have, I want to have.'

The effect of this is that imitation very often contains within itself a hidden form of conflict. In our ordinary social and psychological world it already *is* conflict. When Satan tempted Adam and Eve, he encouraged them to be like God: 'God knows that when you eat of it your eyes will be opened, and you will be like God,

knowing good and evil' (Gen 3:5). In order to be like
God, they had to disobey God. They had to set themselves up over against him, against his will for them –
which was the Good, their own ultimate Good.

We have to learn, then, to understand the danger that
is contained in imitation. We need to understand that
imitation leads to rivalry and that rivalry leads to conflict, both within society and between societies. We also
need to see that Christ offers us a form of imitation that
is without rivalry – his imitation of the Father. If we are
to imitate Christ, it must be done in the way that Christ
imitates his Father. Not 'over against', but simply 'with'.

The imitation of Christ: being where he is

What, then, can be said about the 'imitation' of Christ,
if imitation opens the door to rivalry, to competition, to
a desire to supplant another? Surely the imitation of
Christ is something good in itself? Are we not called to
be like Christ? Christ died as a martyr, as a witness to
the Truth about human beings, about society, and about
the ultimate purpose of creation. And yet the early
Church was quite firm in discouraging its members from
seeking martyrdom. To imitate Christ wilfully and in an
outward manner is not the way of God. It is not even the
way of Christ.

What did Christ himself do? We know that he did
what the Father does, that he spoke the words that the
Father gave him to speak, that he judged as the Father
judges – but he did not do this in an external manner.
He did it because the Father was *in* him: 'The Father is
in me, and I in him' (Jn 14:11). There is no opposition
here; there is no 'over against'. Christ and the Father are
one. How can this be? It is possible because the Holy
Spirit also dwells in Christ. The Spirit of God the Father
– the Spirit that proceeds *from* the Father – rests on the

Son. Indeed, the Spirit lives within the Son. The Spirit *abides* in him. Both Father and Spirit act from within the Son with one accord and in unity with the Son. There is no external imitation here. There is oneness of life and oneness of will. What Christ does as the incarnate Son of God is what the Father and Spirit *want* him to do – and what *he* wants to do. Christ does not do what the Father and the Spirit have done elsewhere in some other situation. God never repeats himself. Whatever God does is always new and whatever Christ does is always new.

We ourselves, then, do not need to try to imitate Christ in any external sense. Our outer path will never be the same as his. We are called to act from within at the prompting of God dwelling in our hearts: Christ within us, and the Spirit within us. And if Christ is within us, then the Father – of whom Christ says, 'the Father is in me, and I in him' – will be in us as well. We will have been reconciled with the Father. Jesus tells us not to worry when we are threatened or under pressure from without: 'When they bring you before the synagogues, and the rulers and the authorities, do not worry about how you are to defend yourselves or what you are to say; for the Holy Spirit will teach you at that very hour what you ought to say' (Lk 12:11). We can be sure that what the Spirit tells us will be something new. There will be no question of our imitating anyone else at that moment. We will be ourselves, acting and speaking at the prompting of God.

To meet Christ truly, then, we must join him where he is. And where is he? Not just here with us, in us, but also on the throne he has occupied from the beginning, from before the foundation of the world. This is the significance of Ezekiel's vision:

> And over [the living creatures'] heads there was something like a throne, in appearance like sapphire;

and seated above the likeness of a throne there was
something that seemed like a human form (Ez 1:26).

The prophet has seen the Son of God *before* his
Incarnation. He is *already* sitting on his throne above the
heavens. This Son and Word of God, one 'that seemed
like a human form', in the fullness of time descended to
become the incarnate Christ and to meet us where we
are.[2]

We ourselves, however, will not truly meet Christ
where he is and as he is in the fullness of his being, until
we ourselves have ascended to where he is, until 'the
Son of Man is seated on the throne of his glory' and
those who have followed him also 'sit on twelve thrones
judging the twelve tribes of Israel' (Mt 19:28): in other
words, until we have come 'to the measure of the full
stature of Christ' (Eph. 4:13). Only then will we have
that 'knowledge of the Son of God' of which Paul in
Ephesians speaks (Eph 4:13): not just knowledge *about*
the Son of God, or even the knowledge that comes from
a personal relationship with the Son of God, but the
knowledge that the Son of God has of the Father and of
the world.

How many have met Jesus in this way? How many
have joined him where he is? I think we can confidently
say: very few. The Apostles, after the Resurrection, and
no doubt some of the saints. But for the rest of us that
meeting still lies in the future. Nevertheless a foretaste
of it is available to us now. It is 'on offer', for Christ has
appointed it to all those who will follow him in his
temptations, in his trials (cf. Lk 22:28–30). I suppose
that the reason we have not yet joined him in this way is
that we have not yet truly followed him, we have not yet
stood by him. Much lies ahead of us, yet what lies ahead
is part of the promise, part of the covenant God has
made with us: if we will follow him, we shall see – and

share in – his glory; we shall meet him – and join him – where he is. The scale of this is shown by the prayer said just before the beginning of the divine Liturgy: 'In the grave with the body, in Hell with the soul as God, and in Paradise with the thief, and on the throne with the Father and the Holy Spirit, wert thou, O Christ, filling all things, thyself uncircumscribed.'[3]

4

Seeing the World through God's Eyes

Right at the beginning of Jesus's ministry as described in the Gospel of Luke, there is a crucial point at which he makes it clear for the first time that he is the Christ, the Lord's anointed, and the saviour of Israel. It is the Sabbath Day and Jesus goes into the synagogue to pray. Everything starts well. He offers to read, is duly chosen by the leader of the community, opens the scroll handed to him and reads a portion of Isaiah:

> The Spirit of the Lord is upon me, because he has anointed me to preach good news to the poor. He has sent me to proclaim release to the captives, the recovering of sight to the blind, to set at liberty those who are oppressed, to proclaim the acceptable year of the Lord (Lk 4:18; Isa 61:1–2).

We do not know if this was the appointed passage for the day, or if he simply opened the book at that point.

In any case, Jesus closes the book, hands it back, and says to the people: 'This day is this scripture fulfilled in your hearing.' In other words, he applies Isaiah's words to himself – a shocking thing to do, to say the least. At first the congregation 'marvelled at the gracious [i.e. 'grace-filled'] words which proceeded out of his mouth'. Yet in their wonder and amazement they soon asked themselves: 'Is not this Joseph's son?' – 'Is he not just one of us?'

At that point Jesus changes the tone of the encounter. He seems almost deliberately to provoke their envy, with the suggestion that he will not be doing in Nazareth the miracles they heard he had done in Capernaum, a rival city not many miles away – and he anticipates their reaction: 'No prophet', he says, 'is accepted in his own country.' Why? The examples Jesus gives are extremely illuminating.

First, he reminds them about Elijah. There were many widows in Israel in Elijah's day, for it was a time of hardship and famine, and yet Elijah was not sent by God to one of them, but to a widow in Sarepta, far up the coast near Sidon, in the land of a non-Jewish, Canaanite people. God sent Elijah to a woman outside of Israel, and it was *her* son whom Elijah brought back to life. It was *she* whom God cared for through the prophet, not one of his – the prophet's and God's – own people. From the point of view of the probably all-male congregation in Nazareth, this person was truly peripheral. First, she was not Jewish, second, she was a woman, and third, she was a widow, someone without great weight in society – and possibly dangerous.

Just in case his hearers do not understand, Jesus offers them Elisha as a second example. In spite of the fact that there were many lepers in Israel, Elisha cleansed through his prayer the flesh of Naaman the

Syrian. Naaman, too, was an outsider, and yet God was interested in him. It is at this point that anger wells up in the hearts of Jesus' audience. They simply cannot accept to be told that God might be interested in *others*, in people not like them, in people not 'ours', in people at the margins of – or even outside – the society in which they live and with which they feel at one.

It would appear from the Gospel account that Christ deliberately provoked this reaction in them. He knew how they could be expected to react to what he was going to say – and he said it anyway. In doing so, he was giving them a chance to see what was in their hearts – and to change – but his hearers did not grasp the primary, fundamental truth of the 'good news': that God is equally concerned about us all. He has no favourites. He 'shows no particularity' (Acts 10:34) – or in the older, and perhaps more powerful translation, he is 'no respecter of persons'.

Seeing in order to believe

The worshippers in Nazareth were provoked to anger by what they saw and heard in the synagogue. On another occasion, when Christ heals the man who has been blind from birth, he causes not so much anger as confusion. 'Some of the Pharisees said, "This man is not from God, for he does not observe the Sabbath." But others said, "How can a man who is a sinner do such signs?"' (Jn 9:16). This was a very unusual healing. Others had raised the dead, cured leprosy and performed 'mighty acts' with the assistance and at the prompting of God's grace, but as the Gospel itself tells us, 'Never since the world began has it been heard that anyone opened the eyes of a person born blind' (Jn 9:32). Yet this is just what Christ does. In fact, he opens not only the eyes of the blind man's body, but of his mind and heart. So too he is able to take the heavy 'givenness' of each of our lives and move it on, not only at the physical, bodily level, but at the level of the soul, of the inner person.

What is even more interesting, however, is what this miracle means for the disciples, for it is clear from the narrative that Jesus intends that they, too, should learn something – should *see* something – as a result of it. This is apparent right from the beginning, when the disciples ask him, 'Rabbi, who sinned, this man, or his parents, that he was born blind?' Jesus answers, 'Neither this man nor his parents sinned; he was born blind so that the works of God might be revealed in him' (Jn 9:2–3). Clearly, in Christ's eyes the disciples were looking at the situation from entirely the wrong angle. They were looking for guilt. In Christ's eyes – in God's eyes – this man's blindness did not point to the past, to previous failings or sins, but to the future. Indeed, ultimately it points forward to the Kingdom of God.

What Christ does here is to show the providence of God that is reflected in all that takes place in a world that is constantly moving forward. The providence of God is present in what happens to us and to others, whether it seems to our eyes to be good or to be bad. There is a modern tendency, one that goes back several centuries and has its roots in Greek philosophy, to think of this world as somehow the product of the interplay between chance and necessity. What happens to us has no meaning in itself, no meaning other than what we as observers give it. But in Christ's eyes nothing could be further from the truth. Meaning and relevance are built into the world, and it is our task to grasp them – and to act accordingly. In the story of the man born blind, Christ discounts the effect of sin on the blindness of the man and declares that his blindness occurred 'that the works of God might be revealed in him'. We should

conclude, then, that even this man's blindness is somehow included within the providence of God.

What, though, are these 'works of God' to which
Christ refers? In the first place, God is at work so that
the man may live life more abundantly – in this case,
through having regained the proper use of his eyes.
Secondly, the work of God is that he should come to see,
with the inner eyes of his soul, that Jesus is not simply
an itinerant miracle worker, but 'the Son of Man', 'the
Man'. Thirdly, it is that having seen this, he should
believe in Jesus as the Son of Man and worship him.
John brings all this together in just a few words:

> Jesus heard that they had driven him out [of the
> synagogue], and when he found him he said, 'Do
> you believe in the Son of Man?' He answered, 'And
> who is he, sir, that I may believe in him? Jesus said
> to him, 'You have seen him, and the one speaking
> with you is he.' He said, 'Lord, I believe.' And he
> worshipped him (John 9:35).

The man born blind, then, both sees and hears the Son
of God become the Son of Man, and goes on to worship
him. This is the goal set by God for each one of us, the
goal of the whole of creation as it relates to us personally, and as God sees it. 'I came', Christ says, 'that they
may have life, and have it abundantly' (Jn 10:10). The
only thing that stands in the way of this process, and
prevents the achievement of this goal, is human sin.

The scale of what is taking place in this miracle is
immense: creation itself is shown to be a providential
act, designed to bring into existence, out of nothing,
personal entities – 'hypostatic' entities in the language
of theology – that can enter into a personal relation with
their Creator. Creation is designed to bring *us* into existence and to provide the framework not only for our

existence, but for our eternal existence, our eternal life, through divinisation, by sharing directly and personally in the life of the Creator, in the life of God. Nothing that exists – and therefore nothing that happens – has any other goal or aim. The most distant galaxy exists for this, and is intimately bound up with what we are and what we are called to be. The only aspect of creation that is not working for our salvation is that portion of it which has been distorted by human sin. All the rest is an expression of God's love for us, and of his desire that we should all be saved.

If we were to look at the case of the man blind from birth from a modern medical perspective, we would probably say that his condition was largely or even entirely due to chance: the chance modification of a gene connected with the development of the eyes would be enough; or the chance contracting of a particular disease by his mother during pregnancy. The realm of chance, however, operates only at the superficial levels of creation, while the deep structure of the world, the divine *Logos* that carries the form and meaning of all that exists, is unaffected by chance. It persists throughout, and continues to reflect God's providential will, which is that we might 'have life, and have it abundantly'.

As a result, at every point in the story of each one of us, our being opens out at its deepest level onto salvation, and onto the coming Kingdom. All we need to do is to 'see': to see what the thrust of our lives should *really* be, in which direction, at the deepest level, God wants us to move, and to use the freedom he has given us in order to move along that path. That way forward, that path, always exists deep within us at every moment. The effects of chance may obscure it, but chance cannot wipe it out or eliminate it from creation.

Even if we are born blind, even if, as the result of sin, our lives are a mess, God still *wills* that we should be saved, and that will is reflected, for each one of us, in the deep structure of our lives themselves, in the very 'givenness' of our being. It may be hidden from us now, or at any particular moment, but Christ has come specifically to 'give sight to the blind' and to enable us to see and thus to find that pre-formed, providential path that will lead us to salvation.

What we find in the Gospels is that we are constantly being asked to look beyond what is immediately visible to our senses. It is only by doing this that we can make the vital connections and find the *logos* that will enable us to believe. While the disciples are sitting at table, during their last meal together with Jesus (Judas has already left to meet with the guards who will arrest him), Philip says, 'Show us the Father, and we will be satisfied.' Jesus replies, 'Have I been with you all this time, Philip, and you still do not know me? Whoever has seen me has seen the Father' (Jn 14:8–9). The *logos* that links Christ and the Father can be seen in the face of Christ for those that have the eyes to see. This in itself would be enough for Christ to be called and to be the 'Word' or *Logos* of God. In the face of Christ and in his words, the Father speaks.

After the resurrection, Thomas is asked to place his hand into Jesus' side and not to doubt but to believe. He places his hand in Jesus' side, and exclaims, 'My Lord and my God.' but Jesus makes no reference to this striking gesture. Instead he says, 'Have you believed because you have seen me? Blessed are those who have not seen and yet have come to believe' (Jn 20:29). For those with 'eyes to see and ears to hear' the presence of Christ was enough to enable them to see God and to believe in him. Even in Christ's day, however, many were unable to 'see' what was before their eyes or to 'hear' his words, just as many others have been able to 'see' Christ and 'hear' him with the eyes of faith long after he ceased to be physically present on earth.

Seeing with the eyes of faith

The mere presence of Christ among us, then, is not enough for us to see with eyes of faith. If we return to the reaction of the worshippers in the synagogue at Nazareth, the truth of the matter is that the hardness of heart that rose up in the hearts of Christ's listeners is present in all of us. All that is required are the appropriate circumstances, and it will appear, because we still have not 'seen' the Father as revealed to us in Christ. We all – to the extent that the kingdom of God has not broken into our hearts – construct our world on the basis of 'them' and 'us'. There is always *someone* whom we are tempted to exclude, whom we seek to marginalize, whom we want to peripheralise. This will be someone whom we place outside *our* world, and whom we therefore assume to be outside *God's* world, outside the area of his concern.

Time and time again in the Gospels, Christ shows us that this is not the way the Father sees the world. The Father's perfection is revealed, according to Christ, in the way he is concerned for all. God 'sends rain on the righteous and on the unrighteous', and 'makes his sun to rise on the evil and on the good' (Mt 5:45). There are no marginal people from God's point of view. Each and every one of us is 'centre stage': each and every one of us receives the same attention and love.

The roots of this central aspect of the teaching of Christ can already be found in the earliest scriptures of the Church. Yet we find ourselves again and again separating ourselves from others for one reason or another, and when we do this, we constantly try to enlist God as a witness on our side. Christ came, in part, to tell us that we cannot do this; that God does *not* accept the constraints that we put on our relationships with others, but is more open, freer, than we can ever hope to be.

5

Members of One Body: the Crisis of Baptism

The Eucharist, as we have seen, creates the Church, uniting us into one body – the Body of Christ. Becoming a member of the Church, however, is not an instantaneous event. It is a process that takes place over time. In the Early Church the normal way of entry into the community was through adult baptism, which involved a period of preparation, a catechumenate during which instruction took place. People were taught, tested, and then finally baptised, chrismated, and admitted to communion.[1] A good percentage of us these days were baptised as children, and have no personal awareness of this process as it affected ourselves. In some ways this is unfortunate, since becoming a Christian involves a certain kind of personal crisis. In a sense, without experiencing some sort of crisis no one can become a Christian at any stage of their life, whether they were baptised as a child or not.

We tend to think of a crisis as a decisive moment, a moment in political, economic or personal life that brings with it the potential for change. The normal meaning of the word *krisis* in Greek, however, is actually 'judgement', and we very often find it translated as 'judgement' in the New Testament. Our current use of the word 'crisis' in English, however, seems to go back to another meaning of the Greek word, one which actually comes from the medical literature. It is found first in Hippocrates in about the fifth century BC, where a *krisis* is the turning point in a disease, a change for the better or for the worse. It is the point at which the disease either develops in a way that leads to the patient's recovery, or in a way that means they will not recover. This is the moment of crisis.

When we find ourselves in a crisis, not only have we often been placed there by forces outside our control, but also we find that decisions have to be taken. If you are a doctor, those decisions have to be taken on the basis of an understanding of what is required at that moment to help move a person in one particular direction or another. So judgement is required, but it is not so much the judgement of a judge in court, as a form of *discernment*, that involves knowledge of what needs to be done. There is a very important saying of Christ in the Gospel of John that relates to this. Jesus is talking to his disciples and to the Pharisees and says, 'Now is the judgement (*krisis*) of this world; now shall the prince of this world be cast out' (John 12:31). It is as if Christ is identifying a critical moment in the progress of the disease that we call history, and is predicting that it will turn for the better – the prince of this world shall be cast out. This applies very clearly to the whole movement of our lives in relation to the sacrament of baptism, and it is very helpful to consider the baptismal service from this point of view. [2]

The sacrament of baptism as celebrated in the

Orthodox Church today is much the same as in the Early Church, at least from the third or fourth centuries. It has three parts. First there is a section that assumes the existence of the catechumenate, a period of preparation that involves renunciation of the fallenness of this world. In this part of the service, the candidate is received as catechumen. Then there is the baptism itself: the washing away of sin through incorporation into the death and resurrection of Christ. Finally there is the service of chrismation, which can be understood as a form of personal Pentecost, the gift of the Holy Spirit into the heart of the believer that brings with it the possibility of newness of life.

The reception of a catechumen

At the very beginning, when the person who wishes to be received as a catechumen is brought into the church, he or she faces towards the east, that is, towards the rising sun, the source of light as it dawns upon the world. This is not without significance. Christ himself is the Light that has dawned upon the world, the Sun of righteousness, and so it makes liturgical sense to face east as if to greet him. The priest breathes three times on the candidate, and signs him or her three times with the sign of the Cross. This breathing reminds us of the end of the Gospel of John (Jn 20:22), where Christ comes to the disciples after the Resurrection, breathes on them and says, 'Receive ye the Holy Spirit.' Already, at the very beginning of the process of becoming a member of the Church, the Holy Spirit is involved. By the priest's breathing three times, and signing with the sign of the Cross three times, we are also reminded that the Trinity is involved from the very beginning. There is no movement towards Christ that does not involve all three persons of the Trinity. There is no movement at all without the Holy Spirit, and there is no presence of the Spirit that is not at the same time Trinitarian.

The priest then also places his hand on the head of the person who is seeking to draw nearer to Christ. At once we should ask ourselves, 'Where else does this kind of gesture take place?' – and, of course, it happens in ordination. To become a catechumen is to enter the 'order' of catechumens, an order of the Church, and so the priest places his hand on the person and admits him or her to that order. Now the candidate always comes to the church accompanied by a sponsor. Where else are sponsors required? In the sacrament of marriage.[3] No one enters an order of the Church without the support of others. No one is a Christian on their own. As in marriage – and in ordination to the diaconate, the priesthood or the episcopate – we are brought forward and supported by the community or its representatives.

The service of baptism then continues with prayers read over the catechumen. In the first of these the priest says, 'I lay my hand on thy servant, *N.*, who has been found worthy to flee to thy holy Name...'. God has already been active in this person's life by bringing him or her to this point and it is ultimately God himself who judges the person worthy. Our personal opinion in the matter is of no great significance. The priest then goes on to ask God to 'remove from him his former delusion'. This is a powerful comment on the former life of the catechumen, a comment on the past, and on the world in which he or she has lived. We enter an area where judgement and condemnation are involved, and where new perspectives, new understandings, are brought into play. There was a former life that was a life of delusion, and God is asked to remove that delusion.

At this point, the idea of a change of behaviour is also introduced. God is asked to enable the catechumen to 'walk in all his commandments', that he or she 'may find life in them', may find eternal life. Not only is new light cast on the nature of the world and its fallenness, but also the prospect of new life – a new form of life – appears. God is, in fact, asked to inscribe this person in the 'Book of Life'. In the Early Church there would have been a list of catechumens, just as there would have been a list of baptised members and a list of clergy. People who were received into the order of the catechumens were inscribed, in that 'order', in the Book of Life, not only in heaven but on earth. The whole process is a movement that involves not only the individual, not only the Church, but also God, for ultimately it is God who has brought this person to this point.

One really gets into the heart of the process of baptism, however, with the exorcisms that follow. We are not, these days, used to referring frequently to the devil, or to Satan, or even to 'the evil one', in our ordinary lives.[4] Yet we are all aware that evil is present in this world, whether in disguise or openly, and this same realisation marks the whole of the baptismal process.

In these exorcisms the priest asks the Lord to rebuke the devil: 'Christ came into the world that He might overthrow thy tyranny and deliver mankind.' It is Christ's desire that we should be freed from the tyranny of the devil, and thereby saved. How did Christ overthrow the tyranny of the devil in the first place? He did so on the Cross. The baptismal service uses the same imagery as is used by St Paul in Colossians: '[Christ erased] the record that stood against us … nailing it to the cross. He disarmed the rulers and authorities and made a public example of them, triumphing over them in it' (Col 2:14–15). Christ defeated death on the Cross, and now leads Satan and his company in the triumph, like a victorious general. It is Christ who by death has destroyed death and overthrown 'the one who has the power of death, that is, the devil' (Heb 2:14). As a result, 'death no longer has dominion over him' (Romans 6:9). The defeat of death is bound up with the overthrow of the devil on the Cross.

There are three prayers of exorcism in the service that is in use today, but it is clear from the early Church orders going back into the third and fourth centuries that, in some places at least, it was the practice to exorcise again and again. All those who had been admitted to the catechumenate were expected to come to church during the week, and at the end of the service the priest or bishop would exorcise them. Why? Because 'Satan will not be able to conceal himself for ever.' He will have to reveal himself in the course of these repeated exorcisms. This will not only enable the individual to detect the presence of evil, but will enable the community to judge whether he has truly turned from his former ways. In the first prayer, in fact, the priest addresses Satan directly and says, 'Fear, be gone, depart, and do not hide thyself in him (*her*)', thereby implying that it is quite possible for Satan to conceal himself in us.

It is very important to realise that the Fathers of the Church who wrote these services – and the Church in which they were developed – had a view of the world in which what cannot be perceived by the senses is more important than what can be seen. The most complete account of the nature of this unseen world is found in the work of Dionysius the Areopagite.[5] He names nine orders of angels that form a hierarchy between human beings and God, and who mediate to us the goodness and power of the Creator. These nine orders are actually mentioned in the first baptismal exorcism, directed at the devil: 'Fear thou God ... before whom tremble Angels and Archangels, Thrones, Dominions, Principalities, Authorities, Powers, the many-eyed Cherubim and the six-winged Seraphim ...'. Some of the angels belonging to the lowest order have ceased to obey God. It is these that have taken up their abode in our hearts. The priest asks that these hidden evil powers should 'depart from this sealed and newly enlisted warrior of Christ'. The new catechumen is 'sealed' in the sense that he or she has been marked with the sign of the Cross, and is 'enlisted' by having his or her name placed on the list of catechumens. Now they are warriors of Christ, having entered into battle with the 'adverse powers'.

The second prayer of exorcism makes it quite clear, however, that ultimate power in creation remains in the hands of God. It refers to 'Jesus Christ, who has all power in heaven and on earth'[6] and has foreordained for Satan 'the penalty of eternal punishment'. It also tells the devil to 'depart from him (her) who has made himself (herself) ready for holy Illumination'. Illumination is something that is not simply given to us without any effort on our part. It is something for which we must prepare ourselves by a certain way of life.

In the third exorcism the priest asks God, 'who heals every malady', to 'root out from him (her) every operation of the devil'. He asks God to 'rebuke the unclean spirits' and 'speedily crush down Satan' under the catechumen's feet, so that he or she may be made worthy 'to partake of thy heavenly mysteries'. Thus this whole process is seen as a struggle against 'unclean spirits', against dark spiritual powers that are abroad in the world, and God is asked to join the catechumen in fighting them. It is also a process of illumination, in that the person who has presented himself for baptism has come to see the true nature of this world. Evil is present in it and is a power which must be taken seriously. To do battle with it we will require God's assistance.

After these three exorcisms we move on to a prayer that begins by referring to the fact that God has created Man in his own likeness, and has bestowed on him the power of eternal life. We were not created for death. We were created for life. We were created in the image and likeness of God, so that the life of God might find a home in us. After the Fall, God has provided salvation for the world through the Incarnation. Why? The service makes this clear: in order to free us from bondage to the enemy, and to enable us to enter into the heavenly kingdom. For this to happen, however, we need understanding, discernment, and so the priest asks God to open the eyes of the understanding of the catechumen, and 'yoke unto his (her) life a radiant angel who shall deliver him (her) from every snare of the adversary'. Again we see here the presence of the unseen world. We all have a guardian angel, whether we are aware of this or not, and the prayer asks that this angel be brought into the closest possible relationship with our lives, that he be 'yoked' to us and join us in our fight against Satan.

The priest again breathes on the catechumen, pointing to the constant presence of the Holy Spirit in this whole process, and at the same time he says: 'Expel from him (her) every evil and impure spirit which hides and makes its lair in his (her) heart.' This he does three times. We see here that our bodies are not only temples in which the Spirit of God can dwell. They are also a home for evil and impure spirits that can hide themselves there. Entry into the Church is a process designed to makes us aware of this fact and lead us to choose to become 'children of the Light'. The first Epistle of John says quite simply: 'God is Light' (1 Jn 1:5). If this is so, to be a child of the Light is to be a child of God. We are also called to become heirs of the kingdom of God. To be an heir is to look forward to an inheritance that has not yet been received. To be an heir orients us towards the future, but towards an inheritance that will only be available to us if we live in accordance with the commandments of God.

The service then moves on to a personal renunciation of sin. Throughout all this the community of the Church is praying over the catechumen and now, finally, the person to be baptised is asked to renounce Satan personally, to renounce 'all his angels, all his works, all his service and all his pride'. He or she is turned towards the west, away from the source of Light, and having repeated the renunciation of Satan three times, is invited to breathe and spit on him so as to show outwardly a personal turning away from the evil one. The catechumen has recognised the enemy and now proceeds to expel him, to breathe him out and to spit on him. In a similar way, having now turned back towards the east, the catechumen is asked three times, 'Do you unite yourself to Christ?' and then, finally, 'Have you united yourself to Christ?' After the catechumen has answered all these questions in the affirmative, the priest says, 'Bow down also before him.' The catechumen's response is: 'I bow down before the Father, and the Son, and the Holy Spirit, the Trinity, one in essence and undivided.' Not just before Christ, but before the Trinity. Only then is he or she asked to recite the Nicene Creed, for it is only *in* and *through* the Spirit that one can know Christ as King and as God. It is only *in* and *through* Christ that one can truly know the Father.

In the final prayer before the baptism proper the priest asks God to 'call thy servant to holy Illumination'. Baptism is a process of illumination, of gradually increasing insight into the nature of God and into the nature of the world. It invites us to 'put off your old nature which belongs to your former manner of life' (Eph 4:22) and to be renewed and set on the path to everlasting life. God is asked to 'fill him (*her*) with the power of the Holy Spirit, in the unity of thy Christ'. In other words, God is asked to make this person a member of the Body of Christ, the Church.

The baptism

As the baptism itself begins, there is a distinct change of emphasis. There is much less reference to Satan, and the positive elements – the gifts that come to us through baptism – come to the fore. Once again this is seen as a process. We pray that person to be baptised may not only be illumined by the light of understanding, but that the water may also be effectual 'for the averting of every snare of enemies, both visible and invisible'. Again our attention is drawn to the unseen world. The priest prays that the person to be baptised 'may prove himself a child of the Light' and 'may be a member and a partaker in the death and Resurrection of Christ our God'.

At this point we enter the very heart of this process, the critical moment – the 'crisis' point – in our movement forward: our entry into the death and Resurrection of Christ. The priest asks that he or she 'may be a partaker of the death and resurrection of Christ' and asks God to 'create the image of thy Christ in him (*her*) who desires to be born again'. To create in us the image of Christ is to re-create in us the image of Adam – the first Adam – who himself was created in the image of the Son of God. Re-create this person, we ask, put him in touch with his or her true nature as willed by God. Enable him or her to start again, to be born again. This is what God desires.

There follow the prayers over the water, which have

an extraordinary cosmic character. God 'upholds creation' and has 'joined together the universe out of four elements'. 'All powers tremble before him; the sun sings to him, the moon glorifies him, the light obeys him ... '. At the same time the prayers stress God's love for us: 'Thou couldst not endure to behold mankind oppressed by the devil.' The Incarnation is the response of God's love and his desire for our salvation. Christ himself, in his coming, blessed 'the streams of the river Jordan, sending down upon them from heaven his Holy Spirit, and crushed the heads of the dragons that lurked therein.' In the waters of this world there are still dragons – demons – that need to be crushed. Christ's baptism in the Jordan achieved this, and our baptism in Christ extends the process. We pray that this water will be 'the final destruction of demons, unassailable by hostile powers, and filled with angelic might'. The destruction of demons continues to take place in the Church through the blessing of the baptismal waters and their use in the rebirth of all those who enter into membership of the Church. These waters are now filled with angelic might, with invisible power, with the power of God mediated to us through creation.

The purpose of these prayers is clear: 'Let all adverse powers be crushed beneath the sign of the image of thy Cross.' The priest blesses the water with his hand three times and breathes on the water three times, again expressing outwardly the invisible presence of the Spirit and of the Holy Trinity. What he seeks to do – and what *we* seek to do – is to crush these adverse powers with God's help. How? By the image of the Cross, and ultimately by the Cross itself. In baptism, then, we first ask God to cleanse the water of all that is dark, and then plunge the person to be baptised into that same water, inviting God to use it to cleanse him or her of that same

darkness. We ask that for the person who is being baptised this may be a critical moment, a 'crisis' in the
medical sense of the word, when the disease that affects
us turns decisively in the direction of healing.

Chrismation

The service of chrismation that follows is for 'the averting of every assault of the devil'. Again we assume the
presence of invisible evil powers in the world and ask
God to protect us from them. It invites us to enter upon
a struggle in which we are involved already, whether we
know it or not, and from which, with God's help, we can
now hope to emerge victorious.

In the introductory prayer, the priest asks God to
'keep him (her) in thy sanctification' and 'deliver him
(her) from the evil one and from all the machinations of
the same'. We have to expect that Satan will continue to
be active against us. Afterwards, when the oil of chrismation is being wiped off (originally on the eighth day,
but now normally at the end of the service) we ask God
to 'maintain the shield of his faith unassailed by the
enemy' (the word for 'enemy' is in the plural here, referring to the demonic powers) 'and maintain *unassailed*
the pledge of the Spirit'. We have to expect that the gift
of the Spirit will attract the attention of the enemy. And
finally we ask God to keep this person 'unconquerable
in every attack of those who assail him – and *us*'. In this
way all who are present at the service are encouraged to
accept that the struggle against evil into which Christ
entered and emerged victorious is also our struggle, and
will continue throughout our life in the Church.

Thus we see that the catechumen has, through baptism, entered upon a struggle between Satan and Christ
that is taking place on a vast scale. God's final victory is
assured, but in order to contribute to it we will need

first to accept that it is taking place. Our aim is to follow the commandments of Christ, which will enable us to have a chance, at least, of overcoming Satan. Belief in Christ and faith in him underpins all of this. Belief leads to discernment, which leads in turn to a willingness to follow Christ, and this opens to us membership in the community of those who are being saved. We, too, triumph over the powers of darkness, but we do so by entering into the Church through the Cross and Resurrection of Christ. Death, in the context of baptism, is the door to rebirth into newness of life. Through baptism and chrismation we become Spirit-bearers. We are anointed and become followers of the Christ, the Anointed One. We have no reason to believe that our struggle with the enemies of Christ will ever cease in our lifetime. We have entered into it, we have recognised its nature, and we have called on God to help us. We have seen that Christ has been victorious, and we seek to be victorious through the same means as he was victorious – through the Cross.

'The judgement of this world'

Now we can see what Christ means when he says: 'Now is the judgement (*krisis*) of this world; now shall the prince of this world be cast out.' Through Christ's commitment to the Cross, Satan is overthrown. We in turn are offered a chance to cast out the prince of this world from our own lives, but this involves that same kind of commitment to life through death and resurrection. It is at the point of commitment that victory is won. This turning point, the 'crisis', will follow us throughout our lives. If Christ was able to say just once, 'Now is the judgement of this world', we must expect to have to repeat it again and again. We can only do this if we have entered into Christ's way of looking at the world – if we have entered into the struggle into which he entered, if we have accepted suffering as he accepted it, and if we have seen – with him – that the victory over the adverse powers is God's victory and not ours.

6

The Narrow Gate of Forgiveness

In the Orthodox tradition communion is closely bound up with the sacrament of confession. The Greek word for confession is *exomologêsis,* and it means 'to reveal', 'to acknowledge' one's sins. Thus the act of confession falls naturally between repentance, which leads to a desire to confess before God, and forgiveness by God, which is the desired result of confession. In practice it is difficult to separate all these things. They are all important, and each offers an opportunity to look at the whole. Each can be approached through both the earlier and the later scriptures, the sacred texts that antedate Christ and those that reflect his Incarnation. They can also be looked at through the texts of the Divine Liturgy itself. When we look closely at the scriptural texts and stories, we find that forgiveness is closely associated with healing, and healing with both resurrection and love.

Repentance, confession and forgiveness

In the earlier scriptures, forgiveness has two main forms. There is the sacrificial approach, which goes back to the days of Cain and Abel and is systematised in the Law of Moses. In the Mosaic Law sins are specific transgressions of specific commandments. Leviticus 5, for example, lists different transgressions of the Law, and prescribes the various sacrifices, or sin offerings – a lamb, a goat, a turtledove – that can be offered to atone for them. Atonement – the reconciliation with God that is desired by someone who has transgressed the Law – is achieved through sacrifice.

The other strand of forgiveness – the prophetic strand – is perhaps best represented by Psalm 51:[1] 'Have mercy on me, O God, according to your steadfast love; according to your abundant mercy blot out my transgressions ...', and is exemplified by a passage in Jeremiah in which the element of sacrifice seems to have disappeared.

> The days are surely coming, says the Lord, when I will make a new covenant with the house of Israel, and the house of Judah ... I will put my law within them, and I will write it in their hearts; and I will be their God, and they shall be my people. No longer shall they teach one another, or say to each other, 'Know the Lord', for they shall all know me, from the least of them to the greatest, says the Lord; for I will forgive their iniquity, and remember their sin no more (Jeremiah 31:31–34).

The prophet looks forward to a 'new covenant' and definitive reconciliation with God seems to be located in the future. At the same time, atonement and reconciliation with God are associated with a new and deeper knowledge of God, 'for they shall all know me ... and I will remember their sin no more'.

This is an extremely important passage, and it provides a strong link to the scriptures that mention Christ. In particular it points to the prophecy of Zacharias, the father of John the Baptist, who says of his son:

> And you, child, will be called the prophet of the Most High; for you will go before the Lord to prepare his ways, to give knowledge of salvation to his people by the forgiveness of their sins (Luke 1:67, 76–7).

Here, as in Jeremiah, the knowledge of salvation – and therefore knowledge of God – is associated with forgiveness. It is not surprising, then, that John the Baptist went about preaching the 'baptism of repentance for the forgiveness of sins' and that the people who went out to be baptised by him did so 'confessing their sins' (Mk 1:4–5).

The sequence of repentance, confession and forgiveness appears here quite clearly, and the preaching ministry of Christ is bound up with this same process, though there the stress turns towards repentance. We read, for example, that 'after John was arrested, Jesus came to Galilee, proclaiming the good news of God, and saying, "The time is fulfilled, and the kingdom of God has come near: repent, and believe in the good news"' (Mark 1:14–15). This preaching of the coming kingdom is at the heart of Jesus' ministry, and preparation for entry into the kingdom involves repentance.

Forgiveness, healing and resurrection

When we look closely, however, at what Christ actually does when he forgives people their sins, we find that there is a close and consistent connection with healing.

An important miracle in this respect is that of the paralysed man in Mark 2. The man could not move, and his
friends bring him to Christ lying on his bed. They
actually break through the roof of the building in order
to do so. When Christ sees the faith of the man, and of
his friends bringing him, he says to him, 'My son, your
sins are forgiven.' This in itself is striking. A man is
lying there unable to move, and Christ forgives him his
sins.

The scribes who are watching say to themselves, 'This
is blasphemy!', since to their minds only God can forgive sins. Jesus perceives what they are thinking and
asks them, 'Which is easier, to say to a man, "Your sins
are forgiven", or "Rise, take up your pallet and walk"?'
His question implies that he thinks everyone would
agree that the latter is greater than the first. But is it?
Other itinerant miracle workers had no doubt healed
people who were paralysed. Clearly humans can do such
things, even if they do need God's help. For most people
living then – and now – healing the sick man would not
be considered greater than forgiving him his sins. But
what if both acts are divine, in the sense that both are
anticipations of the transformation of this world in the
last days?

Raising a man and causing him to stand upright is a
clear pointer to the resurrection of the dead, and resurrection to eternal life is the goal of human history and of
the story of the universe as a whole. All of Christ's
miracles point to this coming transformation in one way
or another, particularly the raisings of Jairus' daughter,
of the son of the widow of Nain, and of Lazarus. In each
of these, resurrection breaks in to this world, just as it
does in the raising of the paralysed man from his bed.
Resurrection, then, can be added to the sequence of
repentance, confession, forgiveness of sins and healing.

The raising of the paralysed man tells us that healing follows on from the forgiveness of sins. The forgiveness of sins is something *on the way* to healing, which is itself an aspect of the coming resurrection.

This is why healing is greater than the Sabbath itself, as Christ shows when he heals the man with a withered hand on the Sabbath day in Mark 3. The story of the raising of Jairus' daughter in Mark 5 implies the same thing, but it has another story inserted within it. While Jesus is going to Jairus' house to heal his sick daughter, a woman in the crowd around him touches the hem of his garment. Immediately she is healed of a disease that had afflicted her for twelve years. Jesus notices what has happened, and turns and tells her, 'Your faith has made you well.' While this is going on, Jairus's daughter actually dies, and when Christ comes to the house mourning has already started. Nevertheless, he brings her back to life. The structure of the story itself suggests that healing is something that precedes resurrection – or better, that resurrection somehow includes healing, just as the healing of the woman with an issue of blood is included in the story of the raising of Jairus' daughter.

Repentance, confession, forgiveness and love

The relationship between forgiveness and love becomes clear in the story of the woman who anointed Christ's feet with precious ointment and wiped them with her hair (Luke 7:36–50). This takes place in the house of Simon the Pharisee, where Jesus has gone to have dinner. A woman known to be a sinner comes in with an alabaster box of ointment. She stands behind him at his feet, weeping, and then begins to wash his feet with tears and dry them with her hair. She kisses his feet and anoints them with the ointment. This is scandalous. This woman might also be ritually impure, so that Christ is allowing a situation to develop that is very difficult for everyone present.

Simon says to himself that if Jesus were really a prophet he would have known that this woman was a sinner and kept away from her. Christ reads his thoughts and tells him a story of two debtors, one of whom was forgiven a debt of five hundred denarii, and the other a debt of fifty. Which of these, he asks, would love the man who released him from his debt more? Simon answers correctly, 'I suppose he to whom he forgave more.' Jesus then points out the difference between the way Simon greeted him – no water for his feet, no kiss, and no oil for his head – and the way the woman greeted him. 'Therefore I tell you,' he concludes, 'her sins, which are many, are forgiven; hence she has shown great love.' It is not that because she loved much, her sins were forgiven, but that her great love is clear evidence that her many sins have already been forgiven.

This sequence of events is similar to what we have seen before: an implied but unseen repentance, leading to acknowledgement of sin, which leads in turn to forgiveness and ultimately to love. The effect of this is to introduce love between forgiveness and resurrection and to place it alongside healing. Forgiveness is bound up with all these things. It would appear that forgiveness is the gate not only to healing and resurrection, but also to love.

The forgiveness of others

This brings us to another crucial point. Christ clearly links our forgiveness by God to our forgiveness of others. This is absolutely central to his teaching. It even appears in the Lord's Prayer: '… and forgive us our trespasses, as we forgive those who have trespassed against us.' If the path to forgiveness passes through the narrow gate of repentance and confession of sin, then it also passes through an even narrower gate: the forgiveness of others. In Mark's Gospel Christ goes so far as to say, 'Whenever you stand praying, forgive, if you have anything against anyone; so that your Father in heaven may also forgive your trespasses' (Mark 11:25). This includes, of course, forgiving our enemies. How many times should this be done? When Peter asks this question, Jesus tells him, 'Not seven times but, I tell you, seventy times seven' (Mt 18:22) – and he probably means for the same sin, repeated again and again.

One has to be ready constantly to forgive. The parable which follows after this last saying of Christ is that of the unforgiving servant, a man who is let off an immense debt of ten thousand talents, and then demands repayment from someone who owes him a hundred pence. When his master hears about this from the other servants, he is angry and hands him over to be tortured until he has paid all that he owes. 'So,' concludes Jesus, 'my heavenly Father will also do to every one of you, if you do not forgive your brother or sister from your heart' (Mt 18:35).

The same teaching is found in Luke: 'Do not judge, and you will not be judged; do not condemn, and you will not be condemned. Forgive, and you will be forgiven' (Luke 6:37). The centrality of Christ's teaching on the forgiveness of others could not be more strongly stressed than in the story of the crucifixion. Of all the words of Christ from the Cross, there is only one that refers to the teaching he has been giving to his disciples: 'Father, forgive them, for they do not know what they are doing' (Luke 23:34). Of all the commandments he has given them, this is the one he reminds them of as he is dying.

Forgiveness and the Divine Liturgy

Forgiveness also plays a part in the story of the Last Supper, which is taken up and completed in the Eucharist. The Markan account is a very stark text:

> While they were eating, [Jesus] took a loaf of bread, and after blessing it, he broke it, gave it to them, and said, 'Take; this is my body.' Then he took a cup, and after giving thanks he gave it to them, and all of them drank from it. He said to them, 'This is my blood of the covenant, which is poured out for many' (Mk 14:22–24).

Matthew adds to 'poured out for many' the phrase 'for the forgiveness of sins' (Mt 26:28). As soon as he does that, of course, we are immediately taken back to Leviticus and the world of sacrifice, where we link up with the older of the two strands in the understanding of forgiveness that are found in the scriptures that ante-date Christ. The effect of this is to make Christ himself the sacrificial offering that brings about atonement for the 'many', that is, for the people. It is only on the annual 'Day of Atonement', of course, that sacrifice is offered for all the people. At other times, it is offered on behalf of individuals.

When it comes to the Liturgy, Matthew's 'for the forgiveness of sins' is applied to the bread as well, so that we say 'that is broken for you for the forgiveness of sins.'[2] So, as in the ancient sacrificial system of Israel, the offering of a pure and guiltless victim brings about the forgiveness of sins. In the Liturgy of St John Chrysostom it is striking how frequently the reference to forgiveness of sins occurs in the prayers that are usually read in a low voice by the celebrant (and therefore are not normally audible to the congregation). For example, the whole emphasis in the 'First Prayer of the Faithful' is on the forgiveness of sins:

> We thank thee, O Lord, God of the powers, who hast counted us worthy to stand even now before thy holy altar and to fall down before thy compassion for our sins and those things done in ignorance by the people. Receive our prayer, O God; make us worthy to offer thee prayers and supplications and bloodless sacrifices for all thy people.

And in the 'Second Prayer of the Faithful':

> Cleanse our souls and bodies from every defilement of flesh and spirit; and grant us to stand without guilt or condemnation before thy holy altar ... Grant that, always worshipping thee with fear and love, they may partake of thy holy mysteries without guilt or condemnation, and be counted worthy of thy heavenly kingdom.

Just before the Great Entrance, when the Holy Gifts will be brought through the church to be placed on the altar, the celebrant says to God:[3]

> Look down upon me, thy sinful and unprofitable servant, and cleanse my soul and heart from an evil conscience. And, by the power of thy Holy Spirit, enable me who am clothed with the grace of the priesthood to stand before this, thy holy table, and celebrate the mystery of thy holy and most pure Body and thy precious Blood.

Then, in the offertory prayer, God is addressed in a similar fashion:

> O Lord, God Almighty, who alone art holy and dost accept a sacrifice of praise from those who call upon thee with all their heart, accept also the

prayer of us sinners and bring it to thy holy altar, and enable us to offer thee gifts and spiritual sacrifices for our sins and for those things done in ignorance by the people.

Clearly the offering of the Liturgy as a whole is intended to bring about atonement with God for all the people through the forgiveness of sins. We are reminded at once of the Jewish liturgy for the Day of Atonement as described in detail in Leviticus 16.

After the consecration of the bread and wine, forgiveness of sins is linked several times during the Liturgy to avoidance of 'judgement and condemnation'. The priest prays that communion – partaking in the consecrated Gifts – may be 'for vigilance of soul, remission of sins, communion of thy Holy Spirit, fulfilment of the kingdom of heaven, freedom to speak in thy presence, and not for judgement or condemnation'.

Again, in the prayer during the litany before the Lord's Prayer, the priest ask God to:

> ... count us worthy to partake of thy heavenly and dread mysteries at this sacred and spiritual table with a pure conscience, for remission of sins, for forgiveness of offences, for communion in the Holy Spirit, for inheritance in the kingdom of heaven, for freedom to speak in thy presence, and not for judgement or condemnation.

Then, when introducing the Lord's Prayer, the celebrant says in a loud voice: 'And count us worthy, O Master, that with boldness and without condemnation we may dare to call upon thee, the God of heaven, as Father, and to say, "Our Father …"'.

It is not at all clear to what these words 'not for judgement or condemnation' and 'without condemnation' can mean, unless they refer to the phrase, 'forgive us our trespasses as we forgive those who trespass against us' in the Lord's Prayer itself. All the other petitions of the Lord's Prayer are straightforward requests directed to God. Only one concerns what *we* must do, and this is — 'as we forgive those who trespass against us'. In saying this prayer and going forward to receive communion afterward, we are submitting ourselves, in effect, to God's judgement as to whether we do indeed 'forgive those who trespass against us'.

These expressions, 'without condemnation' and 'not for judgement or condemnation', follow us to the moment of communion itself, reminding us that there is something we must do if we are to receive communion worthily, and that is to forgive those who have offended us. At the very last moment, in the prayer recited before receiving communion, we say:

> Count me worthy to partake without condemnation of thy most pure mysteries for the remission of sins and for eternal life ... Not for judgement or condemnation be the partaking of thy holy mysteries unto me, O Lord, but for healing of soul and body.

In this way a connection is also made between forgiveness of sins and the 'healing of soul and body'. A 'deep structure' is present here that reflects the teaching of Christ in the Gospels. The forgiveness of sins, preceded by repentance and acknowledgement of one's failings, is the pathway to healing, not just of the soul, but 'of soul and body'. As in the Gospels, forgiveness by God affects the whole person. It is a stage on the way to bodily resurrection and eternal life.

Behind the stages along the path that leads to eternal life is an understanding of the need for God's forgiveness. Repentance is one of the narrow gates through which we approach forgiveness. But forgiveness of others – including our enemies – is a second and even narrower gate through which we must pass. As we see in the life of Christ, the forward movement that leads to inner – and in Christ's case, also to bodily – resurrection can be experienced in this life only through the forgiveness of others. Repentance has two results. One is the acknowledgement of one's own sinfulness. The other, as we see already in the story of John the Baptist, is change in the way we live. In the context of Christianity, it also leads to baptism.

Thus baptism 'for the forgiveness of sins' takes its place as a stage along the path leading to our full integration into the death and resurrection of Christ. It makes of us members of the Body of Christ. But it is never the end of the story. Full integration into life in Christ, the assimilation of our lives to Christ's self-sacrifice, is not something easy to achieve, for it not possible without the forgiveness of our enemies, which is the gateway to true love.

Section 2

Difference, Division and Healing in the Life of the Church

7

The Mystery of the Church

The words 'for healing of soul and body'[1] that are spoken before communion point to the way in which the human being is an embodied whole. We don't expect God to work only on our souls or only on our bodies. But what does it mean to be a 'body'? How does the 'body' relate to God?

We tend to think of the world as existing only in its visible aspect, but for the ancient philosophers and for the Fathers of the Church creation has *two* fundamental aspects. There is the visible aspect that can be perceived with our senses, and the invisible aspect that is just as real – and, in some sense, more real – than the visible, but cannot be perceived by the senses. This distinction goes back to Plato and beyond, and is fundamental for understanding the theological tradition and even the liturgical practice of the Eastern Church.

Though these two fundamental aspects of creation

form a single, completely integrated and unitary whole, their relationship to each other is nevertheless a mystery. The scientific developments of recent centuries have revealed more clearly than ever before a strange and apparently insoluble problem: the radical discontinuity between our perceptions and what we discover behind them through scientific investigation. Although we perceive colour as, for example, red, or green, when we look at colour from a 'scientific' point of view, what we find is waves of energy. These waves, however, are not themselves coloured. They have nothing to do with what we think of as colour. They do have form and energy, but *as* form and energy, they are not capable of being perceived by our senses.

The same is true of sound. We hear sounds of quite extraordinary variety, with different pitches, overtones, timbres, intensity – but scientific investigation reveals that behind these sounds there are also waves of energy. Again, we do not perceive the waves as waves: we only perceive the sound. In order to perceive a sound *wave*, you have to create a piece of equipment that will convert it into something you can actually see. Sound waves can be transformed so as to be perceptible to our sense of sight – but to see a sound wave is not to hear it. The same is true of smell and of taste. We now know that taste and smell are determined by the shape of the molecules involved – yet yet what we smell is not a shape. What we taste is not a shape. We relate directly to the 'real' world that surrounds us through sight, taste, smell, hearing and touch. None of these, however, exists in three dimensions.

On the other hand, when we try to get behind a perceptible phenomenon such as sound or sight, therefore, we do find another reality, one that we can grasp with our minds but cannot perceive with our senses unless it is first converted into a visible form. Understanding the perceptible world is difficult enough – but it is simplicity itself when compared with the invisible, imperceptible world whose structures of form and energy the scientist investigates. This discontinuity was already known to Plato in the fourth century BCE, and the Church Fathers were completely aware of it. It was an ordinary part of their philosophical and scientific culture.

The *Logos* and the deep structure of creation

The deep structure which lies behind the perceptible world – and which we can grasp with our mind – is related to what we refer to when we speak of Christ as the 'Word' or '*Logos*' of God. We do not have access to that invisible, imperceptible realm of the world's deep structure through the senses, though we can draw near to it though the *nous* – but we can be certain that it is very, very different from our ordinary world.

By the fifth century, the general understanding of the Fathers was that everything that exists in creation is conditioned by its *logos* or its 'deep structure'. This deep structure is not something that we humans construct for ourselves simply through a consideration of outward appearances and the application of the reasoning power of our own minds. It is an inbuilt created form that reflects God's purpose for any created thing. The sixth-century theologian Dionysius the Areopagite, when speaking of these same *logoi*, calls them the *thelêmata*, or the 'wills' of God. They express God's providence in creation and are intimately related to God's purpose in creating the world in the first place. According to Maximus the Confessor, an outstanding theologian of the seventh century, the *logos* of any created thing contains three elements: its coming into being (*genesis*), its movement or development (*kinêsis*), and its eschato-logical point of stability in God (*stasis*). From another point of view, Maximus the Confessor can speak of a '*logos* of being', a '*logos* of well-being', and 'a *logos* of eternal being' that exists for every creature. The first relates to God as the primal Cause, the second to God as the Good and therefore as the foundation of all move-ment and change, and the third to God as the 'hidden attractor' and goal of all movement and development in an eschatological perspective.

The *logos* of each created entity is not just the prin-ciple of its existence, its movement and development. It is also the source of differentiation in creation. Differ-ence exists in the world because God has willed this to be so. It also distinguishes God from creation, in that in God, difference in this technical sense does not exist. In creation it is the norm, while the unity and oneness of God is complete, not even affected by the existence of the three Persons, each of whom is somehow *in* the other. The *Logos* of God, identified with the Son, the Second Person of the Trinity, contains in himself all the divine *logoi* on the basis of which creation was formed, and holds them together in a unity that trans-cends them all. Thus for the Christian, contemplation of the *logoi* of created things leads to an understanding of their oneness in God, and through this to an under-standing of the oneness of the *Logos* of God in his relation to the world.

What I have been describing thus far has been a world without sin. Since the Fall, however, the relation-ship of human beings (and some of the angelic powers) to one another and to God has been seriously distorted. They are no longer one with each other and with God in the same way. A new element has entered the world: division. Division in this technical sense is something

made possible by our freedom of choice. We can separate ourselves from each other, and from God, in such a
way as to cease living in accordance with our God-given
logos through which our difference from God and from
each other is reconciled and overcome. We can acquire a
'mode of being' (*tropos hyparxeôs*) that is contrary to our
'deep structure' or 'true nature'.

The role of the Church

After the Fall, it is in Christ, the incarnate Word, that
this separation is first overcome. Having brought God
into the world in a unique and personal way through his
own Incarnation, Christ then moves to extend that victory by creating the Church, his extended Body, which
is called to be light in the darkness of fallen humanity.
The vocation of the Church, then, is to increase, and
eventually fill that darkness with God's light, pushing
back the darkness and reducing the extent of its power.
The Eucharist is the point where, in the life of the
Church, one sees most clearly the way this process
works: the entry of God into the world through Christ,
and the communication of his light to the members of
the Church.

Given our understanding of creation, however, we
can see that the Church will always exist in a state of
tension with the darkness of the fallen world around it.
There is no other way for it to live. If it is at one with
the surrounding culture, then you can be sure that the
darkness of that surrounding culture has entered into
the Church. This is a very important point, and should
colour our perception of the place of the Church in history. The other conclusion we should draw is that the
Church's vocation to expand belongs to its very nature.
Missionary activity is of the essence of the Church,
which has been called into existence by Christ with the

intention that it should expand and eventually embrace the whole of mankind.

Thus the Church as the mystical Body of Christ, with ourselves as members, with all the physicality that we as humans possess in this created world, is carrying on the work of Christ among mankind. There will always be fallen elements within the Church. Every period in its history shows this to be true, and the line of demarcation between the Church and the surrounding darkness is not razor sharp. That outer darkness can also be found within the Church, while at the same time, the light of Christ is present outside it. After all, at the time of Christ's Incarnation, the Church as we know it had not yet been born – and yet there was light. Justin Martyr, one of the early Apologists, made this point very clearly, when he referred to Socrates, Heraclitus and others as Christians because they 'lived with reason [*logos*]' even though they lived before the birth of Christ.[2] There is, nevertheless, a border between the Church as the Body of Christ and the world outside it, defined and preserved by its canonical structures.

The presence of darkness within the life of the Church as we experience it does not, and cannot, however, affect its deep structure, which is rooted in creation as willed by God. The deep structure of the Church is founded upon the deep structure of creation – and as a result, it cannot be shaken. This is why the 'gates of hell cannot prevail' against the Church (Mt 16:18). Peter's confession of Christ as the Son of the living God has created a synergy between God and human beings that cannot be overcome, since its foundation is the truth of the created world itself in its relationship to God.

The calling of the Church, then, is to spread the presence of Christ, the experience of the risen Christ that is lived out in the Church and which it is the task of the Church to disseminate throughout the human race and throughout the world. The presence of Christ as the Son of God is simultaneously also the presence of the Father and the Holy Spirit. In the incarnate, embodied Christ, the Holy Trinity seeks to drive back, with the help of mankind, the realm of darkness that has existed in creation since the Fall.

The church building as an icon of salvation

The traditional Byzantine church building can itself be understood as the universe made small. It is the universe brought down to our scale so that we can relate to it directly.

Normally the walls and ceiling of a Byzantine church would be covered with frescoes, as in older Western churches, where the schema is very similar. There is almost invariably a dome in the middle of the nave, and in case you do not grasp the significance of the dome, it may be painted blue and it might even have stars painted on it. In the centre of the dome there is usually an icon of Christ the Pantocrator, the ruler of all. As you move down the sides of the dome, you might find angels surrounding Christ and perhaps the Apostles below them; then further down on the walls will be important scenes from the life of Christ. Finally, on the lower walls and above eye level, you find the saints of the Church. On the floor of the church itself you will find the people of God, the 'saints'. All this is integrated into a single iconographic scheme representing the world, but it is a world in which we have our place, as individuals and as Church. Then, in the apse behind the sanctuary, there is usually the Mother of God with Christ, the Incarnate Word: the same Word of God, who was there at the beginning, creating this world in which we live.

The Byzantine church building is also understood as an icon of the history of salvation. If there is a wall painting of the Last Judgement it is not usually inside the nave or narthex, but in the exonarthex or even on the outside wall, facing outward. Thus as you enter, you would first pass the reminder of the Last Judgement and then enter the narthex, but only afterwards would you pass into the nave, the main body of the church, and find yourself directly under Christ the Pantocrator in the world in the process of salvation. Only the baptised should penetrate this far, while the non-baptised should stay outside, although this is not generally observed today.

Looking forward from the west and along the nave, you would see the icon screen, beyond which is the altar. The icon screen represents the dividing line between this world and the world to come, and also between this world and heaven. It is not, therefore, to be experienced as something opaque, but as something that can be, in a sense, seen *through*. On it you will see the face of Christ, the face of the Mother of God, the faces of other saints. You look through them: you look into the face of a saint and see the face of Christ. You look into the face of Christ and see behind it what is otherwise unexpressed and inexpressible: the person of the Father.

The east-west axis of the church, then, from the west door through the centre of the church into the altar and back again, is an axis along which integration takes place: between God and the world, between heaven and earth, between the invisible and the visible, between Paradise, represented by the sanctuary, and the inhabited earth, represented by the nave. In the course of liturgical celebrations, especially during the Eucharist, the focus of attention moves back and forth. We may start at the west end of the church,[3] but then we move through the narthex and into the nave, penetrating more and more deeply into the reality of the Church, until finally we are focused on the sanctuary, on the age to come, where the consecration of the gifts takes place. Then for communion the gifts are brought back through the central doors of the icon screen into the body of the church. They are offered to God from the world and for the world, and they return to the world as part of the process of salvation, entering this world from the world to come and becoming, in this world, a power drawing us forward to the fulfilment of all things.

In this way salvation history as it is worked out through time is reflected not only in the Liturgy, but in the life of each individual Christian. By offering our lives to God in Christ, only to find ourselves sent back into this world to fulfil our calling as a members of the Body of Christ, we recapitulate the story of Christ himself. As the Epistle of the Hebrews makes clear, through his self-offering on the Cross Christ has entered into that unseen world created by God, and from that world continues to act here in the Church, offering himself again and again in the members of his Body. Thus the church building, as the architectural framework of the Liturgy, does the work of God in symbol and in reality. It binds together the visible and invisible because of the way in which, within the church, the sanctuary represents the invisible, imperceptible world and the nave represents the visible, perceptible world. The church building as a whole brings them into a single unity in which each is related mystically to the other and to the whole.

All this is described by Maximus the Confessor in his *Mystagogy*, or 'Explication of the Divine Liturgy'. He presents his teaching as the coming from a 'blessed old man', who told him what he has written down. This indicates that he is speaking from within the Tradition of the Church, the living tradition that is animated by life in the Spirit, and is not simply telling us his own thoughts. What he says is that the Church, as a building, does the work of God, the work of Christ. It is no co-incidence that Maximus deliberately refers back to the interpretation produced by Dionysius the Areopagite a century earlier. We have in Maximus a picture of a Church which cannot in its essence, in its deepest being, be separated from the world. It is part of the world, bound up with the world as God's creation. The work of Christ in the Church is the restoration of that part of creation that is fallen away from God, to its proper relationship with its Creator – and therefore with the rest of creation. This he seeks to accomplish without interfering with the theological personhood and attendant personal freedom that makes each human being an image of God.

It is not surprising, then, that the two most prominent icons on the icon screen are almost invariably icons of the Incarnation of the Word or *Logos* of God. The incarnate Son of God unifies all things. Thus the icon-screen, with its icons of the Incarnation, represents the point at which all things meet, the point of intimate contact between these various levels of existence: between God and the creation, between the invisible and the visible, between heaven and earth, and between Paradise and this world as we know it now. It is a paradoxical, permeable barrier, permitting those who pray before it to share in both worlds at once, to exist in both worlds at once. Thus it is vital that the icon screen should have doors, so that it is possible, even physically, to move back and forth between these worlds, and in this way express liturgically our union in Christ, who is the union of all. It is through the Incarnation and in Christ that reconciliation and unification with God – at*one*ment – take place.

This is the mystery of the Church: Christ, the Incarnate Son of God, is seeking, through his Body, the Church, to bring back to the Father in the Holy Spirit whatever in the created world has fallen away from God, while all the while preserving our freedom within our vocation as children of God.

8

The Eucharist: Radical Difference and a Common Cup

Unlike division, or separation, difference is built into our world. In fact, Maximus the Confessor singles it out as perhaps the most fundamental aspect of Creation. From the point of view of science the simplest form it can take, that of positive and negative polarity, is built in at its most fundamental levels. One only has to think of the magnet, with its two poles, or the mutual attraction of positive and negative particles, or the conjectural existence of both matter and anti-matter. If you look at the world with the eyes of a physicist, you will probably be inclined, should you find anything that proves to be positive, to look around immediately for something negative to which it corresponds: you simply assume that the world is founded on this or some other very simple form of 'difference'.

For Maximus, the difference between male and

female, man and woman, seems to represent the most complex – perhaps the ultimate – expression of 'difference' in the created world. In this he may well be right. The human being is by far the most complex creature in the universe, and the human brain contains some ten billion neurons, each of which can connect with up to ten thousand other neurons in a network whose complexity staggers the imagination – so the 'difference' between men and women is probably the most complex difference that can be found. Maximus places it in his list of five 'unifications' that Christ came to perform after the separation between God and Creation. The first four are: between the invisible and the visible, between heaven and earth, and between Paradise and this world. Maximus would seem quite justified in letting the difference between male and female represent and somehow sum up all the differences that exist in creation.[1]

What started as difference – 'male and female he created them' – very soon became division, with Adam blaming Eve for his transgression and Eve pointing to the serpent and declaring that he was at fault. This is the beginning of a confrontational relationship between women and men, a 'battle of the sexes' that is division of the worst kind. What we are shown in the New Testament, in the relationship of Christ with the women whom he meets or who become his disciples, is something other. Whatever we may think of Paul's ideas about women, he is nevertheless clear that in Christ 'there is neither Jew nor Greek, neither male nor female' (Gal 3:28). It is this New Testament vision of the relationship of men and women – a relationship of difference without division – that is taken up and developed by Maximus the Confessor.

We have seen how, in the *Mystagogy*, the icon screen of a church represents the permeable barrier between the visible and invisible world, and it is thus the meeting point of the first four differences that must be overcome in Christ. On either side of the Holy Doors, there are icons of the Incarnation. On the left hand side as one looks from the nave there is usually an icon of Christ as a child being held in the hands of his Mother – in other words, in his weakness and humility, the kenotic Christ. On the right hand side, however, you will normally see Christ as teacher or as *Pantokratôr*, the 'Ruler of All'. For all their difference, both are icons of the Incarnation. Looked at from another perspective, however, these icons also represent, in a sense, male and female: the Mother of God with all her tenderness, holding an infant child, on the left as you face the screen, and the Son of God in all his strength on the right. If we then imagine a north–south axis running along the icon screen, we see that the northern end has been assigned to the female and the southern end to the male. Thus it is along this north–south axis that the reconciliation of male and female, if it is to be accomplished liturgically, will have to take place. This is actually what happens in the marriage service: the bride automatically stands in front of the icon of the Mother of God, while the groom stands in front of Christ. The wedding couple mirror in the middle of the church the male–female polarity on the icon screen. This polarity is then transcended in the circular 'dance' they perform around the Gospel in the middle of the church.[2] We do this today without ever thinking about it. No one expects the couple to stand in any other way.

As recently as fifty years ago, of course, this pattern held in the Western churches – there tended to be a women's side and a men's side. At St Barnabas, an Anglo-Catholic Church in Oxford built in the 1860s, the north side of the nave (that is, on the left as you face the altar) is ornately decorated, and the right hand side is blank. Local legend has it that it was agreed that the men were expected to paint their side of the nave, and that the women would paint theirs.

Again, in the *Apostolic Tradition* of Hippolytus, which dates from the beginning of the third century and contains one of the earliest descriptions of the Liturgy that we have, it is said that when the kiss of peace is exchanged the women should embrace the women and the men embrace the men. If you try to picture what would have been taking place, it is hard not conclude that the men and women are standing on opposite sides of the church. Otherwise it is very difficult to imagine just how the kiss of peace would have taken place.

Let us now look more closely at the north–south axis of the church, the one running across the church parallel to the icon screen, and consider what happens at the people's communion. In the Orthodox practice, there is usually only one chalice at communion, containing both bread and wine, and it is usually held by the priest as he stands before the icon screen, just in front of the holy doors.[3] During communion the men and women, who until now have been standing on opposite sides of the church, come together to share in that one chalice. As they do this we see before our eyes, played out in the Liturgy, the unification of male and female that Maximus says is the final unification performed by Christ. Women and men literally come together into one to effect the reconciliation that is offered to them in the one Body of Christ. So far as I can see, this is done unconsciously. You find no references to it in the liturgical texts. It just happens that way.

We seem to have here what has been called by Mary Douglas, the British anthropologist, a *symbolic system*. Symbolic systems exist in all cultures, and structure the

way the members of that culture view the world – and
even how they experience the world. The Byzantine
Liturgy is a profound and extremely developed symbolic
system, which means that it has an internal unity and
cohesion that is not always easy to see. At communion it
is centred on the chalice. It is at the chalice, also, that
the unifications that are expressed along the east–west
axis of salvation are effected, when the priest or deacon
comes out through the holy doors to give communion,
returning to the people their offering now filled with
divine Life. At that moment the unification of God and
the world is effected in the very bodies of those who
participate. For them – and in them – God and
humankind become one, as do the visible and invisible
worlds, heaven and earth and Paradise and this world in
which we live.

It is also at the chalice, however, that the unification
expressed along the north–south axis of the church
takes place, when women and men join together in communion. Because of the nature of the sacrament and its
liturgical expression, this does not take place just at a
'symbolic' level. It takes place in the perceptible world
and in the imperceptible world, in both of which every
Christian lives. It is worth noting that unification can
take place liturgically only because difference has
already been established. The reconciliation between
men and women can be expressed symbolically in their
coming together in the chalice because they are standing
on different sides of the church.

What should now be clear is that the Byzantine liturgy
makes use of 'difference', of our polarised existence, to
express the unifications that Maximus has identified as
being brought about through the Incarnation of Christ.
The existence of a male priesthood inhabiting the sanctuary, marked off from the nave by the icon screen,

means that the nave is almost inevitably seen as some-how female. It represents creation, the visible world, the earth and the inhabited world – and therefore, of course, the earthly Church. The sanctuary, on the other hand, represents the realm of the Divine and the invisible creation, heaven and Paradise. Through communion in Christ the unifications effected by Christ are shared with us, who in the nave represent the created order, the visible realm and the inhabited earth. But the church building – and the Church as the Body of Christ – contains them all, preserving their difference and overcoming all division.

It is worth noting also that at this point the Byzantine liturgy rejoins the liturgy of the Temple in Jerusalem, where on the Day of Atonement the High Priest, having entered the Holy of Holies, comes out to bless the people and effect their reconciliation with God. The High Priest in Israel is inevitably male, while for the Church it is Christ who is the Great High Priest, since it is he who brings about the atonement, the reconciliation and the unification – so far as this is possible – of God and human beings through the forgiveness of sins. This is graphically described in the Epistle to the Hebrews:

> For Christ did not enter a sanctuary made by human hands, a mere copy of the true one, but he entered into heaven itself, now to appear in the presence of God on our behalf. Nor was it to offer himself again and again, as the high priest enters the Holy Place year after year with blood that is not his own; for then he would have had to suffer again and again since the foundation of the world. But as it is, he has appeared once for all at the end of the age to remove sin by the sacrifice of himself (Heb 9:24–6).

If we are to understand, then, why there seems to be such an inbuilt resistance to changing the symbolic use of 'male' and 'female' in the Eastern liturgies we should probably see the cause of this in their functioning as part of a huge symbolic system. This is experienced as internally consistent and is therefore very powerful, setting its mark on the participants' perception of the world without their ever noticing it. Symbolic systems work so effectively *because* they are unseen. This is why we find it so difficult to talk about our own cultures: we do not really know how they work. We can talk about somebody else's culture, but it is very hard to talk critically about one's own. This also probably explains why symbolic systems are highly resistant to change. Each element in them supports all the others. Thus, when you change one element this has a 'knock-on' effect; and so you tend not to change anything: you just let them remain as they have always been.

The other factor lying behind this resistance to change is that symbolic systems are always able to express more than can be expressed by rational discourse. They can be filled with meaning that speaks to the heart and not just to the mind. They are – in the experience of anthropologists – beyond logical analysis, and this is part of their power, their ability to grip human beings and give meaning to their lives at the deepest level.

Without a doubt the Eucharistic Liturgy lies at the very heart of the Christian experience. It is the root from which that experience grows and develops. What we see in it, in its outward expression, is the work of Christ expressed symbolically, in the movement, for example, of the Holy Gifts from the nave into the sanctuary and then back out again for communion. That movement bridges many worlds, bringing them together into one.

It brings together God and mankind; it unites the visible and invisible creation; it makes the kingdom of heaven present on earth; it makes a Paradise of our inhabited world. Finally, closest to home, it effects the unification of male and female, men and women, as they join together in the common Cup. And through them it makes one the extraordinary complexity of creation.

9

Christian Ecumenism: a Dialogue of Difference

If the reconciliation of male and female is the high point and focus of the reconciliation of difference in the created world, there is nevertheless another, perhaps even more complex form of reconciliation that needs to take place if the Church is to fulfil its mission. This is the reconciliation of Christians among themselves, and the realisation in this world of the 'Oneness' of the Church. Again, this is an issue that everyone recognises and yet can do little about. We may all believe in 'One, Holy, Catholic and Apostolic Church', but it is not possible to point to any time in history when this Church actually existed and functioned. From the beginning, to use the language of Maximus the Confessor, difference (*diaphora*) among Christians has led to division (*diairesis*) among them. St Paul found it in Corinth, and he ends up writing to the community there and saying: 'I appeal to you, brothers and sisters, by the name of our Lord Jesus

Christ, that all of you should be in agreement and that there should be no divisions among you; but that you should be united in the same mind and the same purpose' (1 Cor 1:10).

What is the source of this impulse towards division? And how can it be overcome? The history of the Church produces countless examples of division. Efforts were made over the centuries to deal with them, but it was not until the twentieth century that a general feeling emerged that it was necessary to pursue unity on a broad scale. What came to called the 'Ecumenical Movement' began at the beginning of the century and has continued to develop today. While most of the Churches involved were products of the Protestant Reformation, the two largest Churches, Roman Catholic and Orthodox, also eventually began to speak to one another in spite of their troubled history.

Orthodox–Roman Catholic dialogue in the twentieth century

One characteristic of Orthodox–Roman Catholic ecumenical endeavour in the 1960s and 1970s was a tendency to divide the ecumenical encounter into a 'Dialogue of Love' and a 'Dialogue of Truth'. The 'Dialogue of Love', it was thought, would precede and introduce the 'Dialogue of Truth'. In this way it was hoped that in the end it would be possible to reach a situation in which both sides were 'speaking the truth in love' (Eph 4:15). And indeed, there was movement in this direction. After the initial rapprochement between Patriarch Athenagoras and Pope Paul VI in 1965, the two leaders proceeded to a mutual lifting of the anathemas of 1054. For the first time since the Council of Florence in the fifteenth century, a formal process of theological dialogue between the two Churches was established by Pope John Paul II and Patriarch Demetrios I of Constantinople. A Joint International Commission for the Theological Dialogue between the Roman Catholic Church and the Orthodox Church was established in 1979 and it met for the first time on Patmos and Rhodes in 1980.

A series of important and constructive meetings then took place.[1] By 1990, however, history – in the form of the collapse of communism and the granting of religious freedom to the previously repressed Eastern-rite Catholics – was beginning to catch up with theology.[2] Orthodox–Catholic rivalry in the Ukraine reached a pitch where it was hard to see how a resolution could be reached. By the time of the Freising meeting in May–June 1990, where a joint statement was issued declaring that 'we reject "Uniatism" as a means for achieving unity because it is contrary to the common Tradition of our Churches', the situation in Ukraine had deteriorated considerably.

At the last of this series of meetings by the Joint International Commission, at the Balamand School of Theology in Lebanon in 1993, the key issue of so-called 'Uniatism' was again discussed and a joint statement was issued, stressing the relationship of Catholics and Orthodox as 'Sister Churches', with the implication that what was done on any given territory should be done after consultation and, where possible, together.[3]

At this meeting, however, there were no representatives from the Patriarchate of Jerusalem, or from the Churches of Georgia, Serbia, Bulgaria, Greece or the Czech and Slovak lands. The disparity between what was being said in the agreed statements and what was perceived to be happening on the ground in Eastern Europe was so great that the Balamand Statement lost all authority. The 'Dialogue of Truth' had come unstuck and the 'Dialogue of Love' had run into the sand.

Dialogue between the Churches was only renewed at an international level after the election of Pope Benedict XVI in April 2005. A first meeting of the Commission in Belgrade in September 2006 revealed, however, serious divisions of opinion among the Orthodox as to the role of the Ecumenical Patriarchate in world Orthodoxy. A compromise formula was reached which spoke of 'general councils participated in by the bishops of Local Churches in communion with the see of Rome or, though understood differently, with the see of Constantinople'. This was accepted by all the Orthodox Churches present except the Church of Russia.

At Ravenna in October 2007, however, the Church of Russia withdrew from the discussions in protest over the presence of a delegation from the Autonomous Church of Estonia. Rivalry between these two major Orthodox churches was seriously damaging not only the image of Orthodoxy, but the work of the International Commission.

In general, our understanding of the ecumenical process seems to bypass two important human elements in the ecumenical equation: our propensity for rivalry on the one hand, and, on the other, the importance of what I would like to call 'good-neighbourliness', using an expression (*dobrososedstvo*) of Metropolitan Filaret of Minsk, Exarch and head of the autonomous Belorussian Church within the Patriarchate of Moscow.

Rivalry and human desire

Rivalry consists, fundamentally, in our defining ourselves 'over against' the other – whether this 'other' be God or another human being – rather than 'alongside' the other, as *sharing* a common space, a common life and a common being. Among modern thinkers the person who has contributed most to our understanding of this phenomenon is undoubtedly the French anthropologist and theologian, René Girard, best known, perhaps, for his books, *The Scapegoat* and *Violence and the Sacred*.[4] Girard's fundamental insight is that specifically human desire, which arises in us in the course of evolution, after the virtual disappearance of true instinctual desire, is essentially the 'desire of the other'. This is not desire *for* the other, but desire for what *the other* desires. Human desire therefore proves to be largely the result of what Girard calls *mimesis*, a specific form of imitation in which we unconsciously acquire the desires of another person, make them our own, and desire what he or she desires. The result of this process is obviously envy, jealousy, and rivalry of every kind.

We can understand this easily by performing a 'thought experiment' in the best scientific manner. Imagine a room in which a two-year-old child is sitting on the floor surrounded by toys. He is quite contented, and picks up one toy after the other, plays with it for a moment, and puts it down. Then introduce a second two-year-old into the room. What happens? We all know very well what happens. The second child sees the first surrounded by toys, but the only toy *he* wants is that which is being held at that very moment by the *other* child. And which toy is now the most precious in the eyes of the first child? Why, of course, the toy he happens to be holding. The other toys disappear from his consciousness entirely. What we have here is the revelation of mimetic desire, desire acquired through the appropriation of the desire 'of the other', and the rivalry that it engenders. We are accustomed to think of our desires as being somehow what most characterises us as individuals, but they are not. Our most powerful desires come to us from without, and not from within.

A similar situation is brilliantly portrayed in the story

of Adam and Eve in Genesis 2 and 3, the story of the Fall. The attractiveness of 'the fruit of the tree in the midst of the garden' is bound up with the serpent's suggestion that somehow God wants to keep that particular fruit for himself. And why would God want to keep it from our first parents? Because, as Eve herself could see, 'the tree was good for food' and 'it was pleasant to the eyes, and a tree to be desired to make one wise'. But the serpent goes even further. He himself introduces the notion of rivalry when he tells Eve that eating of the fruit of that particular tree will make our first ancestors to be 'as gods'. He offers them a chance to become the rivals of their Creator, to become gods apart from and over against God.

The serpent's deception is achieved through the stimulation of mimetic desire, of desire 'according to the other', an acquired desire that has to be introduced in the subject because it was not there to begin with. The induced desire of Eve – which is then passed on to Adam – leads to rivalry, to competition – and to estrangement. Not only does eating of the fruit introduce division (*diairesis*) between God and Man, where it had not existed before: it also introduces division between man and woman: Adam blames Eve for his own mistake. It is the 'other' now who is the cause of his problems. Adam and Eve no longer hold in common their status as 'children of God'. Having moved away from God, they have also moved away from one another. Indeed, they no longer hold the world in common, but as individuals.

Beyond rivalry: Christ and John the Baptist

The Week of Prayer for Christian Unity begins each year in late January, not long after the time when the Eastern Churches remember the Baptism of Christ, celebrated on

6 January as the Feast of Theophany.[5] The relevance that this feast has for the pursuit of unity is striking – not as a theological event, but as a human event.

At one level, what we see in the story is simply one man asking to be baptised by another. What is strange is that it is the greater who is asking to be baptised by the lesser. John knows that Jesus is greater than he is. As he himself says: 'I am not worthy even to stoop down and untie the thong of his sandals' (Mk 1:7). More significantly, perhaps, he says, 'I have baptised you with water, but he will baptise you with the Holy Spirit' (Mk 1:8). The texts of the Orthodox service for the Feast of the Baptism stress this point: 'The clay cries out to him who formed him', 'Our Deliverer is baptised by his servant', and, echoing the language of St Paul, 'Wearing the form of a servant, you come forth to be baptised by a servant.'[6]

What does this deliberate self-emptying mean? It seems obvious that Christ is seeking to avoid any rivalry with John. He does not place himself above him, cite his own greatness and say: 'Move aside, so that I can take over.' He places himself below him, and invites John to be for him what John has already been for others, even though as Son of God he has no need to be baptised 'for the forgiveness of sins'. In this way, Christ says, we shall 'fulfil *all* righteousness' (Mt 3:15), that is, the righteousness of God and not the righteousness of human beings, which is so often achieved by positioning oneself 'over against' the other.

John seems to understand what Christ is doing and echoes his attitude: he does not seek to set himself up in rivalry with his master. This is clearly reflected in the Baptist's acceptance that 'he [Christ] must increase, but I must decrease' (Jn 3:30). Rivalry is completely absent from the relationship between John the Baptist and

Christ, even when at a later stage John is puzzled by what Christ is doing and seeks to confirm that his initial intuition was correct (cf. Lk 7:19–23).

Rivalry in the Gospels

This lack of rivalry between the two men is extremely important, especially as the Gospels have a great deal to say about envy and rivalry. It was something that affected the disciples to such an extent that the Evangelists do not seem to have thought they could overlook it. The most obvious example is the story of James and John, the sons of Zebedee, who, according to Mark, come to Christ asking that they be given the right to sit on his right hand and on his left when he comes in glory. The rivalry here is not just between James and John and the other disciples, but also between the brothers themselves. Which of the two will be given precedence and allowed to sit on Christ's right hand, thereby outdoing the other? Needless to say, when the other disciples heard of this they 'began to be much displeased', showing that they are rivals for Christ's affection as well.

It is interesting that at a very early stage in the development of the tradition this teaching about rivalry was already being downgraded. Luke does not include the Markan incident in his Gospel, and Matthew makes a point of telling us that it was not James and John who approached Christ, but their mother!

There is a more positive kind of competition between Peter and John as to who should be first to arrive at Christ's tomb after the Resurrection. John runs faster and gets there first, but Peter is the first to enter the tomb. John, however, then goes in himself, and is the first to see and believe. Were they aware of their rivalry? Probably not. After the Resurrection Peter was still looking over his shoulder at John and worrying about

what his final position would be. After Jesus has asked
him three times if he loves him, and has told him, 'Feed
my sheep', Peter looks round and sees John following
them. 'Lord,' he says, 'what about this man?' (cf. Jn
21:20–22).

What, then, does the Gospel say about desire? In
Girardian terms it says, 'Be aware of the temptation to
mimetic rivalry, and if you are going to imitate, be care-
ful about how and whom you imitate.' Yet imitation is
built into the Christian life. St Paul himself says, 'Be imi-
tators of me, as I am of Christ' (1 Cor 11:1; cf. 1 Th 1:6).
Christ takes the process of imitation a step further when
says of himself: 'I must work the works of him that sent
me' (Jn 9:4). Indeed, he goes so far as to say that 'the
Father that dwells in me, does his works' (Jn 14:10).
Nowhere in the Gospels, however, do we see Christ enter
into rivalry with the Father. Why is this? Because his
desire is born of *good* mimesis, which involves accept-
ing, as a human being and as God, the Father's will for
him. In this way he aligns himself with the inbuilt purpose of creation: *theôsis*, the deification of all human
beings – not over against God or in rivalry with God,
but alongside God and in conformity with God's will.

At this point we once more join Maximus the
Confessor. The will of the Father for every creature is its
logos, the deep, inbuilt structure of its being that guides
its existence from its coming into being and throughout
its existence, until it reaches its providential end. We
have the ability to perceive the elementary *logoi* of creation. Indeed, the development of modern – and ancient
– science is built on this ability. You cannot manipulate
the behaviour of a little machine on Mars unless you
have a very deep insight into the way the universe is put
together, that is, into the way *God* put it together. But
the *logoi* that structure the inanimate world are simplic-

ity itself in comparison with the *logoi* of plants and animals. And the *logos* of a human being is as complicated as the *logos* of the universe itself. Otherwise the Fathers – and Maximus in particular – would not call the human being a *microcosm*, a 'little cosmos', a little universe.

God has placed in each one of us the desire, or *erôs*, that we need in order to move forward and achieve deification. We are inevitably led astray, however, and introduce division (*diairesis*) into the world when we appropriate the *eros* or desire of another – unless that 'other' is God. Only the God-given *logos* of a person is held in unity and harmony with the *logos* of every other person in the *Logos* of God, Christ, the second person of the Trinity. As soon as we turn away from and abandon our own *logos*, we introduce division (*diairesis*) into the world. And we abandon our own *logos* when we appropriate the desire of someone else and pretend that it is our own.

Mimetic rivalry and ecumenism

In a sense one gift of Pentecost was a God-given ability to overcome mimetic rivalry. When it reared its head, as in the conflict between Paul and Peter over how to treat gentile converts, it was settled by returning to the primal unity of the community in a conciliar fashion. In the Byzantine Church, the Feast of Saints Peter and Paul, which is perhaps the most significant feast of the Church's year after the Great Feasts of Christ and the Mother of God, has as its icon the two Apostles embracing one another.

The relevance of all this to ecumenism is immense. The movement for unity in the Christian Church has reached the point where we can work together and are able to hold serious theological dialogues on the issues that divide us. But I do not believe we have yet realised that behind our disunity there lies a huge amount of unacknowledged rivalry.

Going back into history, as far as one can tell the primacy of the see of Rome was accepted throughout the world by the end of the third century, within the broader framework of inter-church relations, of course, that governed the links between individual dioceses at that time. At the beginning of the fourth century, however, the creation by the Emperor Constantine of a second capital, Constantinople, the 'New Rome' (like 'New York' or 'New Hampshire' in the United States), introduced a new factor into the equation. 'New Rome' was adorned by taking statutes and monuments from 'Old Rome', and it must have been apparent very quickly that this 'New Rome' was a serious rival to the 'Old'. It is no coincidence that the first general attempt to fix the canonical prerogatives of 'Old' Rome took place at the council of Sardica (modern Sofia, the capital of Bulgaria) in about 343 AD, less than twenty years after the establishment of 'New Rome'. The original capital of the Roman Empire was threatened by its upstart rival and acted quickly to preserve its position.

The next few centuries were marked by intense rivalry between the great sees of Rome, Constantinople, Alexandria and Antioch, until Alexandria and Antioch were effectively neutralised by the Arab conquests of the seventh century. The second millennium then saw the gradual rise of Moscow as a centre of political and ecclesiastical life. In 1448, perhaps foreseeing the capture of Constantinople by the Ottoman Turks in 1453, a synod of bishops elected a new metropolitan of Moscow without reference to Constantinople, thereby for the first time effectively declaring Moscow to be autocephalous. By the first half of the sixteenth century Moscow was already styling itself 'the Third Rome' in rivalry both to 'Old' Rome and to 'New' Rome. Its position was strengthened in 1589, when it managed to acquire the status of a patriarchal see.

What is happening in this competition for power across the centuries? From a Girardian point of view it would certainly seem that we have here a series of mimetic 'moments', where one group of people sees and desires what another group has: the combination of both political and religious power.

From the very earliest days of the Church there have been situations where the State has used its power to support the Orthodox Church both within and outside its borders, sometimes persecuting dissident Christians and depriving them of their rights as ordinary citizens. In the Byzantine world the pattern goes back to the Constantinian settlement in the fourth century. Not only was Christianity declared a *religio licita* by Constantine, but from that time on the power of the State started to be enlisted to remove bishops not favoured by the Emperor, and to persecute those who dissented from State-approved religious orthodoxy. Maximus the Confessor, in the seventh century, was one outstanding victim of these policies.[7] There were many more over the centuries.

Even Constantine and his successors were not, however, the origin of such practices. Already the pagan Roman Empire had used State power to defend its interests in matters of religion. Christianity, which was seen by many as somehow essentially hostile to the State, was the object of intermittent persecution from the days of Nero and Domitian to Decius and Diocletian. It is true, however, that imperial practice was seldom standardised and varied from place to place, often depending upon the attitude of local magistrates. In a sense, the crucifixion of Christ at the hands of the Roman authorities can also be treated as but one instance among many of the way in which the Empire defended what it saw as its interests at the expense of the lives of religious dissidents.

Against this background, then, we can see how appropriation of the desire of the *other* leads to desire for what the other *has*. This leads in turn to rivalry and competition, against which theological argument and spiritual exhortation both prove powerless.

Why? Because the source of our desire has not been recognised. It is extremely difficult to admit to jealousy or envy. And when we do, we will probably still not see how they arise. We think that what we want is what *we* want, and do not realise that what we want is what we see the *other* want – and have. If the second child in our earlier 'thought experiment', on entering the room, had seen the first child throw away in disgust the toy he was holding, would he have headed for that toy as the only one he ever wanted, the only one that was desirable? It is highly unlikely.

In this context the famous 34th Apostolic Canon, which belongs to the canonical tradition of both East and West, assumes particular significance. This canon (a 'rule' or 'standard' of behaviour) specifies that in every region the bishops of that region

> should know the one who is first among them, and recognise him as their head, and do nothing outside their own diocese without his advice and approval ... but let not [the first] do anything without the advice and consent and approval of all.[8]

The effect of this canon – and its purpose – is to bring any rivalry between bishops out into the open and then to bring it under control. This canon is the very foundation of the conciliar structure of the Church, which is essential for fostering and maintaining its unity in Christ. The implementation of this canon is not only a way to incarnate the teaching of Christ about rivalry, but also a way of praising God the Holy Trinity. The 34th Apostolic Canon ends with these words: 'For thus will there be concord, and God will be glorified through the Lord in the Holy Spirit, the Father, the Son and the Holy Spirit.'

The theology of the *Logos*, fallen desire and rivalry: three overlapping patterns

We can see here three overlapping patterns reflected in the world in which we humans live: the *logos*-theology of Maximus the Confessor, the Girardian theory of fallen desire as 'bad' mimesis, and the historical developments brought about by rivalry between Churches. They operate on three very different levels, the first in the realm of abstract theology and on a cosmic scale, the second in the realm of our fallen human psyches, and the third in social psychology and the concrete history of this world. The history of inter-confessional rivalry is illumined greatly by the Girardian analysis of desire, and the Girardian analysis of desire can be shown to be consonant not only with Scripture, but with the Fathers.

Christ has come to replace the desire 'of the other' (that is, the false desire that is not our own true desire), with the desires that are built into each of us by our Creator: our desire for God on the one hand, and, through 'good' mimesis, God's desire for the salvation of 'the other'. He has come to replace 'bad' mimesis with 'good' mimesis, with the mimesis of himself, which leads us on inevitably to mimesis of the Father. It is, after all, Christ who says to us: 'You, therefore, must be perfect, even as your heavenly Father is perfect' (Mt 5:48).

Behind the *logos*-theology of Maximus the Confessor there lies a profound acceptance of difference (*diaphora*) as a God-given aspect of creation. In human terms, this means the acceptance of the 'other' person as having a unique inner *logos* that supports and structures that 'other's' relationship with Christ and with the Father – and with us as well. To the extent that I and my 'other' are in Christ, we will inevitably live in harmony, for in Christ our *logoi* are held together in one overriding and ultimately divine *Logos*. To the extent that we depart from our *logos*, so that our 'mode of being' (*tropos hyparxeôs*) departs from our own 'true nature' (*logos physeôs*), we introduce division between us, together with the possibility of envy, jealousy and rivalry. The latter, unfortunately, lie behind the events of much of ecclesiastical history.

The point here is that the scandal of Christian disunity has been largely driven by the 'scandal' of unseen or unacknowledged rivalry. Why unseen? Because it is the very nature of a 'scandal' – in the New Testament sense – that it *is* unseen. The Greek word *skandalon* means 'stumbling-block', something that trips you up as you walk along. The reason that one is tripped up is that the *skandalon* is not perceived. If it were perceived, we would step over it or walk around it. As Church members – and as Church leaders as well – we need to become aware of our propensity to become rivals of one another. We need to take Christ's teaching about rivalry seriously. For Christ the answer was for each to become the 'servant' of the 'other', just as he himself became a 'servant' of John the Baptist at his baptism, having become man in the first place in order to be the 'servant' of us all.

A 'Dialogue of Difference' to facilitate good-neighbourliness

We should note, however, that the acceptance of difference is but a first step. It is not the end of what God has in mind for us. This is achieved, as Maximus insists, only through love. So a 'Dialogue of Difference' really needs to precede the 'Dialogue of Love', which in its turn is the foundation for the 'Dialogue of Truth', since ultimately only through love can we 'come to the knowledge of the Truth' (1 Tim 2:4). The immediate goal of the 'Dialogue of Difference' is simply 'good-neighbourliness', the ability to live on good terms *with* the 'other' – as he or she is. This may not seem much, but it has a profound theological – and indeed cosmo-logical – significance, in that it reveals our ability to live in the world created by God along the lines determined by its own 'deep structure', the divine *logoi*. To under-stand 'good-neighbourliness' and its place in the created world as fashioned by God, we could do worse than remember that, for the Tradition as a whole, the creation is the work of the Triune God. All three Persons of the Trinity are involved in creating and sustaining the world. The Second Person of the Trinity, the Son of God, is thought of, however, as having a special role in Creation as the Word or *Logos* of God. Knowledge of Christ as the incarnate *Logos* or Word of God revealed in the created order is an introduction to the Truth, while knowledge of the holy, life-giving and undivided Trinity is its crown. Knowledge of the Trinity is given only to love, for 'God is love' (1 Jn 4:8 and 16) and is known through love.

10

A Kingdom of Priests

What do we have when we constitute ourselves as 'Church' through baptism and chrismation? We have a 'body' of which each is a member. And whatever may be the variety in the members of that body, as a whole it is one.

One aspect of the 'oneness' of the Church is the way in which each of its members is a priest. The origins of this go far back into the Old Testament, and an extremely important prophecy to this effect is already found in the book of Exodus. When God is about to take Moses up onto Mount Sinai to give him the Law, he tells Moses what he should say to the people. Moses is told to convey to them these words from God:

> Now therefore, if you will obey my voice and keep my covenant, you shall be my treasured possession among all peoples; for all the earth is mine; and you shall be to me a priestly kingdom, and a holy nation (Ex 19:5–6).

Sometimes, as in the NRSV, the expression 'a kingdom of priests' is translated as 'a priestly kingdom', but 'a kingdom of priests' is what the Hebrew says (the Septuagint translates it as 'a royal priesthood', *basileion hierateuma*). What we see here is that God *wants* 'a kingdom of priests'. He tells the people of Israel, even before he gives them the Law, 'If you will truly obey me, you will be a kingdom of priests.'

A similar prophecy is found in Isaiah, in a passage that is possibly even earlier than the passage from Exodus. Again God himself is speaking: 'But you shall be called the priests of the Lord: men shall speak of you as the ministers of our God' (Isa 61:6). This verse comes only shortly after the one that Christ read aloud in the synagogue in Nazareth, when he declared that the prophecy contained in Isaiah 61:1–2 was fulfilled in his person.[1] It is difficult not to believe that Isaiah 61:6 was not also part of Christ's broader understanding of his ministry: the people he seeks to gather around him as his disciples will be 'priests'. This prophecy about a people made up of priests was never realised in the history of Israel before Christ. Only the tribe of Levi was a priestly people, not the whole nation.

Living stones – from people to temple

Similar language is applied to the end of time and the consummation of all things in the Book of Revelation. John speaks of the people as priests in the very first chapter of the Apocalypse: '[Jesus Christ] has made us ... priests to God and his Father' (Rev 1:6). Then in Chapter 5 he describes a vision in which twenty-four elders bow down and say to the Lamb: 'You have made them to be a kingdom and priests serving our God' (Rev 5:10).

Finally in a third passage he says: 'Blessed and holy is he who shares in the first resurrection! Over such the second death has no power, but they shall be priests of God and of Christ, and they shall reign with him a thousand years' (Rev 20:6). In other words, they shall reign with Christ who is the 'king of kings', and serve as priests with Christ, the 'great high priest' (Heb 4:14). Here we see that a priestly and kingly people, a notion that goes right back to at least the fifth century BCE, is understood by John as having been realised in the Early Church, and as something that will go on to reach its fulfilment at the end of time. It is God's will that the Church – and therefore the human race – should be a 'kingdom of priests'. For John this is something that has been experienced already in the life of the Church.

The First Epistle of Peter is addressed to the 'the strangers scattered throughout Pontus, Galatia, Cappadocia, Asia, and Bithynia' (1 Pet 1:1). To these 'strangers' (who are the first Christians) he says: 'But you are a chosen race, a royal priesthood [*basileion hierateuma*, as in the Septuagint translation of Ex 19:6], a holy nation, God's own people…' He also tells us why they have been chosen: '… that you may declare the wonderful deeds of him who called you out of darkness into his marvellous light' (1 Pet 2:9). This 'royal priesthood' and 'holy nation' is also described in that same chapter as being a 'spiritual house': 'Like living stones be yourselves built into a spiritual house, to be a holy priesthood, to offer spiritual sacrifices, acceptable to God through Jesus Christ' (1 Pet 2:5). Here the priesthood, which is normally personal and individual, has been turned into a corporate reality by using the image of a 'house', since a building is necessarily composed of many different parts.

This same word, 'house', is used again and again in the Old Testament to refer to the Jerusalem temple: the 'house of God', the 'house of the Lord', the place where

God is at home, the place where he dwells. Yet Peter is speaking here to non-Jews, to gentiles, who now form part of the people of God and are therefore a 'spiritual house', a spiritual 'temple'.

Similar imagery is used and developed by St Paul. In Ephesians he says:

> For through [Christ] we both [i.e. Jews and Greeks] have access in one Spirit to the Father. So then you are no more strangers and sojourners, but you are fellow-citizens with the saints, and of the household of God, built on the foundation of the apostles and prophets, Christ Jesus himself being the chief corner stone, in whom the whole structure is joined together and grows into an holy temple in the Lord; in whom you also are built into it for a dwelling place of God in the Spirit (Eph 2:18–22).

We can see a transition here from the people of God to the 'household' of God and then to the 'house' of God: from being a community to being a building that proves to be a temple, the 'dwelling place of God'.

Christ applies to himself this image of the Temple in the Gospel of John. After Jesus has driven the money-changers and sellers of oxen, sheep and doves from the Temple, he says in response to protests from the Jews: 'Destroy this temple, and in three days I will raise it up.' The Jews reply, 'It has taken forty-six years to build this temple, and will you raise it up in three days?' John adds parenthetically: 'But he spoke of the temple of his body' (Jn 2:19ff).

Baptism, the source of our priesthood

There is, then, a long series of ideas behind these passages which leads first to the Temple in Jerusalem and finally to the body of Christ himself. This last image is taken up by St Paul in a number of important passages: he is strongly drawn to the idea that the Church is a body. In Romans he stresses both the differences between the various members of a body and the way in which they all work together:

> For as in one body we have many members, and all members have not the same function, so we, though many, are one body in Christ, and individually members one of another (Rom 12:4).

Then in First Corinthians he returns to the same theme, but here he connects it with baptism and the action of God:

> For by one Spirit we were all baptized into one body – Jews or Greeks, slaves or free; and all were made to drink of one Spirit. Indeed, the body does not consist of one member, but of many. ... But as it is, God arranged the members in the body, each one of them, as he chose. If all were a single member, where would the body be? As it is, there are many members, yet one body. The eye cannot say to the hand, 'I have no need of you', nor again the head to the feet, 'I have no need of you' (1 Cor 12: 13–14; 18–21).

The body may have many different parts, but is still one body, and its members need each other. In Ephesians St Paul takes up again the notion of the body and brings it directly into relationship with Christ:

> He that loves his wife loves himself. For no man ever hates his own flesh, but nourishes and cherishes it, as Christ does the church, because we are members of his body (Eph 5:28).

The Church, the body into which we have been baptised, is in fact the Body of Christ. Referring to the relationship of man and woman in marriage, St Paul tells us that the husband is to love his wife as if she were his own body. This is the love, he says, that Christ has for *his* own Body, the Church, the Bride of Christ. If we wish to follow the example of Christ, this is also the love that each of us should have for the others in the Church both individually and as a whole. As the Head of the Church loves his Body, so we, too, as members of the Church, should love *our* Body, the Body to which we belong, the Body of Christ.

We see here the way in which St Paul uses a particular imagery to overcome the problem of the 'one' and the 'many', as he seeks to reconcile the fact that we are many with the fact that we are one in Christ. In the background, of course, there is also the problem of diversity – of difference – and of diverse gifts. St Paul touches upon this on a number of occasions. To begin with he points out all the differences that exist in the Church – the many different talents, the many different gifts, the many different ministries. And yet, he says, there is a fundamental sameness as well:

> For in Jesus Christ you are all sons of God through faith. For as many of you as have been baptized into Christ have put on Christ. There is neither Jew nor Greek, there is neither slave nor free, there is neither male nor female; for you are all one in Christ Jesus. And if you are Christ's, then you are Abraham's offspring, heirs according to the promise (Gal 3:26–29).

Alongside the many differences that exist between the various members of the Church, then, there is still a fundamental oneness, a fundamental identity, in that all have equally 'put on Christ', and at that basic level difference is in some sense abolished. We are all alike in

Jesus Christ. We are all, as Paul says, the descendants, the 'offspring', of Abraham. We are all children of Abraham and of God by faith. We are entitled to ask ourselves, what is this equality that we have all put on?

The first aspect of this 'putting on' concerns the priesthood, and in particular the putting on of Christ in his role of High Priest. This role is developed only in the Epistle to the Hebrews, and this by itself would be enough to make this text one of the most important in the New Testament. In it the author says: 'So also Christ did not exalt himself to be made a high priest; but was appointed by him [i.e. God] who said to him, "Thou art my Son [a reference to Christ's Baptism and the descent of the Spirit], today I have begotten thee" [Ps 2:7]' (Heb 5:5). The author of Hebrews goes on at once to say: 'As he says also in another place, "Thou art a priest for ever after the order of Melchizedek [Ps 110:4]"' (Heb 5:6).

The high priesthood of Christ takes us right back to the Psalms, the perennial worship of Israel and the source of much of the Church's understanding of Christ. This understanding is summed up in the words addressed to the king of Israel: 'The Lord has sworn, and will not change his mind, 'You are a priest for ever after the order of Melchizedek' (Ps 110:4). This same Psalm 110 is actually quoted by Christ in Mark, where he applies it to himself. He has been discussing theology with the Jews in the Temple, and at the end of the discussion he says: 'How can the scribes say that the Christ is the Son of David? David himself, inspired by the Holy Spirit, declared, "The Lord said to my Lord, Sit at my right hand, till I put thy enemies under thy feet"' [Ps 110:1]. 'David himself calls him Lord; so how is he his son?' (Mark 12:35–6).

The words of Psalm 110:4 take us back, of course, to Genesis 14, where Abraham (still called Abram) is returning home after slaughtering the troops of Chedorlaomer, king of Elam. He is met by Melchizedek, king of Salem, who for no apparent reason offers him bread and wine. This same Melchizedek, who was 'a priest of the most high God', then blessed Abraham and in return Abraham 'gave him tithes of all [the spoils]' (Gen 14:20). The significance of this story for the Early Church is made clear in Chapter 7 of the Epistle to the Hebrews, where the author uses it to justify his treatment of Jesus as 'a high priest for ever after the order of Mechisedek':

> This 'Melchizedek, king of Salem, priest of the most high God, met Abraham as he was returning from defeating the kings and blessed him'; and to him Abraham apportioned 'one tenth of everything'. His name, in the first place, means 'king of righteousness [Melki-zedek in Hebrew]'; next he is also king of Salem, that is, 'king of peace'. Without father, without mother, without genealogy, having neither beginning of days nor end of life, but resembling the Son of God, he remains a priest for ever (Heb 7:1–3).

The author of Hebrews takes this psalm, the first verse of which Christ had already applied to himself in the Gospel of Mark, and links the fourth verse to Christ as well, saying that like Melchizedek, for whom (unusually) no father is recorded in the Bible, Christ himself, the Son of God, has no earthly father. He is like Melchizedek in that he too is 'without descent'. Now it is precisely *this* Christ whom we put on in Baptism: Christ the 'high priest for ever after the order of Melchizedek', but also at the same time Christ the *royal* priest – the King of Salem, the 'King of peace'.

Baptism, then, is actually the source of our priesthood. In it we 'put on' the priesthood of Christ, the great high priest. When we 'put on Christ', we put on his priesthood as well. What is more, we *all* become high priests, since we put on not just the ordinary Aaronic priesthood, but the priesthood of the Great High Priest, eternally a priest 'after the order of Melchizedek'. When we put on his priesthood, we also put on his kingship, which belongs to his priesthood 'after the order of Melchizedek'. As Melchizedek was 'king of Salem', that is, the 'king of peace', so we become 'kings of peace' in Christ. During the Last Supper Christ tells the Apostles that they will sit on thrones with him, that they too will be kings (cf. Lk 22:29).

If we put on Christ's kingship, however, we also put on Christ as prophet.[2] And as we take up his role as prophet, we also take up his role as judge (again cf. Lk 22:29). Christ seeks to give us all that is his, and in the life of the Church he gives us all these gifts through our sacramental baptism into his death and resurrection. Through baptism we become members of the 'royal priesthood' that was anticipated in the Old Testament and foreseen in its fullness at the end of the world in the Revelation of John.

11

Christ's 'Allotment'

Words fascinate, and further light is thrown on the nature of our priesthood if we look at the meaning and origin of the word 'cleric', a member of the clergy. The Latin behind our word 'cleric' is *clericus*, and this is simply a Greek word, *klêrikos*, turned into Latin. The Greek word in turn comes from *klêros*, a term used today in Orthodox churches for the place where the choir stands. The original meaning of *klêros*, however, was a 'lot', as in our word 'lottery' or 'allotment'. The way the Greeks and Romans used to cast lots was to have each person take a piece of pottery, write his name on it and put it into a bowl. Then either the bowl was shaken until one lot popped out, or someone reached in and picked one out at random. The piece of pottery told you who had been chosen. The theory was that the gods were thereby involved in the choice, even if it was, for example, the general of an army who was being selected. This might seem a strange thing to do, but we should bear in mind that when a replacement was chosen for

Judas Iscariot, this was done by lot (Acts 1:23–26). Zacharias, the father of John the Baptist, was also chosen by lot to burn incense in the Temple and was therefore in a position to see and hear the angel of the Lord (Lk 1:9). God is involved in the detail of this world as well as in the bigger picture.

The meaning of the word *klêros* can also expand to include the whole process of casting of lots. From that point there is an understandable development in the meaning of the word to 'what is assigned by lot', as in our expression 'an allotment', referring to a parcel of land for growing vegetables that was 'allotted' to the citizens of a particular area. That same word, *klêros*, then becomes, in a very general sense, a piece of land, a farm, or an estate. In other words, it is a form of property that belongs to somebody, something with physical substance – and since land tends to be passed on through inheritance, *klêros* finally comes to mean 'an inheritance', or 'an inheritable estate'. Thus the word 'cleric' has a long history that it is worth bearing in mind when we consider the use of the word *klêros* in the Septuagint.

There is a marvellous passage in Deuteronomy where God, speaking through Moses, says:

> The levitical priests, the whole tribe of Levi, shall have no allotment or inheritance within Israel. They may eat the sacrifices that are the Lord's portion [LXX: 'the fruits of the Lord is their allotment (*klêros*)'], but they shall have no inheritance [LXX: *klêros*] among the other members of the community; the Lord is their inheritance [LXX: *klêros*], as he promised them (Deut 18:1–2: NRSV).

All the tribes of Israel except the tribe of Levi had land allotted to them. They each had their *klêros*. The tribe of Levi, however, was not given land and had no inheritance among the other members of the people of Israel. Their allotted portion was the Lord: 'the Lord is their inheritance, their *klêros*, as he promised them.' But if they have no land, how do they live? This is a serious problem. And the answer is that they live from the Temple. The fruits of the Temple are reserved for the tribe of Levi.

This may not have been carried out in practice, but that was the theory. The point is that the lot, the portion, of the priestly tribe of Levi is the Lord, and they must live from what the Lord provides.

If we want to find out how this meaning of *klêros* applies to us as a priestly people, however, we need to go to the writings of the Church Fathers. There we find that for Eusebius, writing in the first half of the fourth century, Christ has been given 'as his inheritance (*klêros*) angels and archangels ... and ... God-loving souls'.[1] This turns the whole process of inheritance around. No longer is the 'lot' of the priestly people understood to be God, but the people are Christ's 'lot', his 'inheritance'. The Father gives to Christ, as his 'portion' in creation, the angels and archangels − and God-loving souls, presumably souls inclined to believe in and follow Christ. Elsewhere, using the same kind of language, Eusebius speaks of 'the souls that have been allotted to him [i.e. Christ]'[2] − allotted to Christ, that is, by the Father. This notion is not his own invention, since it is actually already found in the Gospel of John, where Christ says: 'I pray for them [his disciples]: I pray not for the world, but for them which thou hast given me; for they are thine' (Jn 17:9).

In the fifth century Cyril of Alexandria describes '[Christ's] personal ... inheritance (*klêros*)' as 'those on earth'.[3] In other words, to Cyril's mind, Christ has been given by the Father not merely the 'angels, archangels' and 'God-loving souls', but the whole human race. In the same vein, in the eighth century St John of Damascus, in his *Hymn on the Birth of Christ*, speaks of Christ's inheritance as the gentiles, who are offered to him by God. This suggests that to his mind the gentiles have somehow replaced the Jewish people, since from a Jewish point of view, the people of Israel are God's 'lot' among all the peoples of the earth. So there is a very important sense in which even today we are the lot of Christ, both as 'those on earth', as those called from among the gentiles, as the 'New Israel', and as 'God-fearing souls'. We have been given to Christ by God the Father as his *klêros*, his portion, his inheritance. This understanding lies behind the priestly blessing at the end of the Divine Liturgy: 'O God, save thy people and bless thine inheritance (*klêronomian*).'

A similar understanding of *klêros* can be found in the First Epistle of Peter, where the Apostle exhorts the elders ['presbyters'] of the community 'to tend the flock of God that is in your charge ... not for sordid gain but eagerly. Do not lord it over those in your charge (*tôn klêrôn,* plural), but be examples to the flock' (1 Pet 5:3). In the Authorised Version. '*tôn klêrôn*' is rendered as 'God's heritage'. Richmond Lattimore, in his excellent modern version of the New Testament,[4] uses 'your charges', and the Jerusalem Bible, in its characteristically prosaic fashion, translates *tôn klêrôn* as 'any group that is put in your charge'. The point to be noticed here is that in the quotations from the Fathers the reference is to all those who have been allotted to Christ, ultimately the whole of mankind, while in the Epistle of Peter those allotted to the 'elders' are the members of a specific community, i.e. the people of God in a specific place.

Each member of the Church is a member of the clergy

All of this leads us to say what Archpriest Nicholas Afanasiev[5] said years ago: that the whole people of the New Covenant belongs to God and constitutes the *klêros* of God. Each member of God's *klêros* is therefore a *klêrikos*, a 'cleric', and thus in some sense a member of the clergy, because each is a part of what has been given to Christ as his inheritance by the Father. Having said this, however, we need to look at what has happened over time, since we don't use the word 'cleric' in this sense. If we trace the development of the meaning of the word, we see that after the fourth century – and in some cases even earlier – the word *klêrikos* comes to be understood as 'clergyman' and is reserved exclusively to the ordained ministry, instead of being applied to every member of the Body of Christ. In his book, *The Church of the Holy Spirit*, Afanasiev argues that we must go back to that earlier meaning. We must all begin once again to think of ourselves as 'clergy', as ordained ministers, simply by virtue of being members of the Body of Christ.

Irenaeus of Lyons, writing at the beginning of third century in *Against the Heresies*, says: '*Omnes justi sacerdotalem habent ordinem*' – 'all the righteous [i.e. all the members of the Church] belong to the sacerdotal order.'[6] This attitude lasts at least until the time of Dionysius the Areopagite in the sixth century, who speaks of 'the holy order of the people'[7] when referring to the whole hierarchical structure of the Church. He can also speak of all who are baptised as belonging to the 'holy hierarchy'.[8] The notion of the 'hierarchy' itself – something to which all Christians belong – is derived from the Greek word *hieros*, which means 'holy, filled with divine power', and thus is related to the word *hiereus,* 'priest'. We have here, then, a complex of meanings that survived at least into the sixth century. Indeed, it has survived to the present day in the deep consciousness of the Church. When we begin to think scripturally and theologically, we quickly realise that the whole of the Church is a holy body, and that the structures within it, bishops, priests, deacons and so on, are structures within the priesthood of a whole people.

One Sunday morning when I was privileged to visit Ethiopia a few years ago, I got up early to go to church (since it is not far from the equator, the Liturgy begins at about six in the morning). As I made my way to the church I had marked out the evening before, I realised that the people who were walking beside me were completely covered with white. The men had long white linen or cotton garments round their shoulders, and the women had pulled them over their heads. It was most impressive. If we ask ourselves why they were doing this, we find wearing white vestments, at least at baptism, is mentioned as far back as Cyril of Jerusalem in the fourth century. In the tradition of Judaism, however, the wearing of white goes right back to the vestments of the high priest.

We usually think of the high priest as wearing very ornate vestments. He did have such vestments, and would wear them in the Temple except on the Day of Atonement, when he went alone into the Holy of Holies. On that day he put on none of his great jewelled garments, but just a white linen cloak and a golden girdle. This was all that was appropriate when one entered the Holy of Holies. Why? Because this was the realm of the unseen, behind the veil, and was inhabited by the unseen powers, the angels. The high priest joined them when he entered that most sacred and hidden place, and it was right he should be vested as an angel when he did so.

In the Jewish apocalyptic literature from the time of Christ, the angelic powers are regularly described as robed in white, and when Mary Magdalene came to the tomb of Christ after the Resurrection, 'she saw two angels in white, sitting where the body of Jesus had been lying, one at the head and the other at the feet' (Jn 20:12; cf. Mk 16:5; Mt 28:3; Lk 24:4). When you saw an angel at that time you expected him to be dressed in white, since he came from that same hidden realm into which the high priest entered on the Day of Atonement. When Christ was transfigured on Mount Tabor, he temporarily entered that same realm, and as he did so, 'his clothes became dazzling white, such as no one on earth could bleach them' (Mk 9:3).

When we are baptised and put on a white garment, we are joining the high priest in entering the Holy of Holies and following Christ in his transfiguration. We are only entitled to do this because Christ himself has become our great high priest – 'after the order of Melkizedek' – and has entered the Holy of Holies before us. We are assimilated to him and put on the same dazzling garment of light that he put on when he ascended definitively to 'sit at the right hand of the Father'. The wearing of white shows that we 'have put on Christ' and become one with him.

That experience in Addis Ababa is an experience of the liturgical realisation of a theological truth. In the Syriac *Didascalia* of the fourth century,[9] there is a description of the Liturgy which says in part:

> After that let the deacons bring the offerings to the bishop at the altar and let the presbyters stand on his right and on his left, like the disciples before their master; and let the two deacons standing either side of the altar carry a fan of fine skin or peacock feathers or cloth, and let them chase away

gently any little flying creatures, that they should not fall into the chalices. And then, let the high priest who is praying inwardly – as are the other priests – dressed in a bright and shining vestment, and standing before the altar, having made the sign of the cross on his brow, say ... (8.12.3–4).

There then follows a description of the prayers of the Liturgy. In this particular liturgical context, only the bishop, as high priest, seems to wear a white garment. Everyone else wears more ordinary clothes. Again it would appear that we have here a liturgical tradition that goes back ultimately to our Jewish roots, to the practice of the Temple, and is being used in the Eucharistic Liturgy to link the bishop with Christ, the one true and eternal high priest.

When Hippolytus of Rome describes the ordination of a bishop at the beginning of the third century he says that immediately after his ordination he becomes the chief celebrant of the Liturgy that follows, in spite of the fact that every other bishop present will be senior to him. We no longer follow this practice, though the ordination does take place near the beginning of the service, before the reading of the Epistle and Gospel. On the other hand, we do ordain to the priesthood immediately before the consecration of the Holy Gifts, so that the newly ordained priest can pray with the bishop and the other priests when the consecration begins – that is, just at that point where he is taking up his role in the Church. Similarly, a deacon is ordained *after* the consecration, so that he can immediately take up his characteristic role of distributing communion. (It is still the deacon who carries the consecrated Gifts through the Holy Doors out to the people.) Thus each of these three orders is ordained for the particular liturgical function that will characterize their life of ministry in the Church.

When does the ordinary believer enter upon his priesthood? Even earlier than the bishop, and *before* the beginning of the Liturgy. According to the earliest liturgical traditions, baptism customarily took place at Easter immediately before the celebration of the Eucharist, and the newly baptized person would then go on to participate in the Divine Liturgy. Therefore he or she should also be thought of as being ordained for a particular role in the Eucharistic Liturgy. The conclusion that must be drawn from this is that every member of the Church has been ordained to offer the bloodless sacrifice. In fact we find this reflected in Origen, writing about 250 AD. In his commentary on the Book of Leviticus, addressing every member of the Church, he says: 'Therefore you have the sacerdotal office, because you are a sacerdotal people, and therefore you ought to offer the sacrifice of praise'.[10] This expression, 'a sacrifice of praise', occurs at the beginning of the anaphora: 'Mercy, peace, a sacrifice of praise.'[11] Although in practice today this is usually sung by the choir, it really belongs to the whole people. All the baptised have this priestly office and have been ordained to offer the bloodless 'sacrifice of praise'.

Being a priestly people

What does this mean for our own self-understanding as Church? Clearly we are a priestly people, a priestly people that fulfils the prophecy of Isaiah, the exhortation of the Book of Exodus, and the expectations of John. We have existed as this body of priests since the day of Pentecost, for, as Peter says, on that day the prophecy of Joel was fulfilled.[12] On that day the disciples are anointed with the Holy Spirit and become 'anointed ones', Christians, for the first time. They are baptised with the Spirit, as was foretold by John when he baptised Christ (Mk 1:8). The descent of the Spirit takes place upon the Apostles, and through them it spreads into the whole body of the Church. That same baptism of the Spirit is carried forward liturgically and sacramentally in the baptism that we still perform, and which, as St Paul says, is a 'putting on' of Christ. The Christ that we put on in baptism is Christ the high priest. Thus, through our integration into the body of the Church, we are given a priestly role that is also a kingly role and a prophetic role. The primary role, however, is that of priest. The gift of priesthood is something that belongs to everybody in the Church and is something that should be assumed by all.

The Church is a historical body existing in time and in space, and each of us spends only a limited number of years as a member of the historical, time-bound Church. We are born into it in baptism and depart from it in death. People appear, they do their jobs, fulfilling their calling as best they can, and then others have to carry the process forward. The Church is in a constant state of renewal – constantly changing while ever remaining the same. We come and we go. We are replaced by others who may be very different from us, but the essence of the Church is unchanging even while it is constantly being renewed. This renewal is being carried out by God, who draws forward towards himself this visible manifestation of the Body of Christ, this extension through time of the Incarnation of Christ, this continuing temple made up of human beings in whom the Spirit dwells.

When we look at the life of the Church in this way and link it with Christ's words, 'Behold, I make all things new', we see that it is Christ himself, acting together with the Father and Holy Spirit, who is behind the constant renewal of the Church. We are part of that process, and we must take it seriously. We need to rise to the level of our own high calling.

Section 3

Becoming a Healing Presence in the World

12

A God-friendly World

An incident described in Luke 17 leads us to question Christ's whole relationship to the created world. As he is going up to Jerusalem by way of Samaria and Galilee he is met by ten lepers who seem to know who he is and ask him to help them. Jesus simply says to them, 'Go, show yourselves to the priests.' The lepers obey, and as they go they find that they have been healed. Only one turns back to give thanks, however, and Luke points out that 'he was a Samaritan', a 'stranger'. Yet his faith had made him whole.

At one level, this story is intended to show us the importance of giving thanks for what we receive; but there is more. One striking thing is the way the ten men were cleansed 'as they went'. Jesus did not touch them. He did not lay hands on them. He simply told them: 'Go, show yourselves to the priests,' and as they went off to do this, they were healed. How can this be? What makes it possible for someone to be healed in this way? Christ does not even pray for them. He does nothing. Yet they are healed, simply by doing what they *should* do, what they were *required* to do according to the Law – for the Law prescribes that a healed leper should show himself to the priests for them to certify that he is no longer ritually unclean.

What is Christ's relationship with the created world, if he can simply make use of the faithful obedience of a sick man in order to heal him in this way? This question is bound up with another, even more basic question: How is it possible for God to become man? Here, too, the issue is the relationship between God, the Son of God, and the created world. For incarnation to take place the created world must be 'God-friendly'; it must be radically open to God, to his presence and activity in it.

This is what the Fathers of the Church concluded. The Fathers tell us that not only is the human being an 'image' or 'icon' of God. The created world itself is an 'icon', an 'image' of God, and an expression of his good-ness and his love. As a result the human being is an image both of the Creator and of creation. As we have already seen, the church building – and the Church as a whole – are, in turn, icons of humanity and of creation. Each reflects the other and each is somehow contained in the other. Human beings, the church building, the Church and the world are designed from the beginning to receive God. But it is in the life of the Church that we and creation meet in oneness with the incarnate Christ. Both we and creation are designed by God to receive God, and the privileged *locus* of this reception is the Church.

How, then, does our membership of the Church relate to the world in general? One does not have to look very far to find in the news some horrendous story about the Church. Whether it's the abuse of children or women, or the constant squabbling over what is right and what is true, or the role played by organised religion in violent conflicts around the world and throughout history, there is almost always something. Faced with this, can anyone, any sensible person, put his or her *faith* in the Church, *believe* in the Church?

The Church we can believe in, can have faith in, is certainly not the empirical Church, the Church we see every day with the eyes of the body alone, the Church as it struggles through history towards its final fulfilment. That Church, as institution, is deeply touched by the Fall, profoundly affected by the discontinuity between what its members believe about mankind and God, and life as they live it. At the same time, however, it is the Body of Christ, the communion of those who have been touched by God and brought into communion with Christ. It is a communion of those who have been not only touched by God, but completely penetrated by God, made one with God, first in Christ, the Son of God become the Son of Man – and then in those who have had the audacity to join themselves to him.

The Church is, and will remain, a mystery, simply because it is a living organism that is simultaneously both human and divine. While this is true at depth, it is not true in our everyday experience, where in the empirical Church the 'human' often seems to predominate, and God and the hidden 'ways' of God are pushed into the background.

There is one area, however, where God is not and cannot be pushed into the background by human sin, and that is in creation. As St Athanasius once pointed out,

> Nothing in creation had erred from the path of God's purpose for it, save only man. Sun, moon, heaven, stars, water, air, knowing the Word [of God] as their Maker and their King, remained as they were made.[1]

We humans, however, have not remained as we were made. Because of the relationship that exists between creation and the Church, the relationship between believer and Church is much the same as the relationship between any human being and the created universe, understood as the Church 'writ large'. In both cases it is possible to experience at times a painful gap between what our role should be and what it is. In both cases the 'deep structure', the invisible underpinning in energy and form, is provided by the Son, the Word of God, and by the Spirit of God, though in the one case the reason for the painful gap is known, and in the other, perhaps unknown.

The created world with all its beauty is the gift of a loving God. Our very existence is a gift – but a gift always calls for something to be given in return, something that reflects the value of the original gift and generosity of the original giver. What gift can we give in return for our existence? Christ refers to this directly when he asks, 'What shall a man give in exchange for his soul?' (Mk 8:37). The answer is already there in the preceding verse: 'For what will it profit a man to gain the whole world, and lose his own soul?'[2] Clearly, for Christ the universe itself is not worth one human soul. The only gift that could even approximate adequacy is the gift of one's 'soul', one's 'life', the gift of one's whole existence. The gift of *my* whole life, as I have lived it, however, will never be a gift commensurate with my existence as created by God. I am not the person I was created to be, and my offering of myself will always be less than I have received.

Has an adequate gift ever been offered? It certainly was in the self-sacrifice of Christ. But it is also important to realise that the *Fiat*, the *Let it be!* of Mary, the Mother of God, which involved the surrender of the whole of her life to the will of God, was just such a gift. Mary had lived her life as it should be lived, in utter harmony with the 'ways' of God. She was at one with the 'deep structure' of her own being and thus with the 'deep structure' of the universe. In her person she enabled the world to be God-friendly, and into this friendly environment God could come. In no other woman – in no other human being – could he have felt completely at home.

The oneness of the human race from the beginning means that Mary's offering of herself is our offering as well. This is spelled out poetically in one of the hymns from the Eastern Orthodox celebration of the Nativity of Christ:

> What shall we offer thee, O Christ, who for our sakes hast appeared on earth as man? Every creature made by thee offers thee thanks. The angels offer thee a hymn; the heavens a star; the Magi, gifts; the shepherds, their wonder; the earth, its cave; the wilderness, the manger: and we offer thee a Virgin Mother, O pre-eternal God.[3]

It is because of this that any true turning to God in faith that is followed by obedience – as in the case of the lepers in Mark's Gospel – brings a person into line, at least momentarily, with the inner workings of God in creation. Faith is thus a potential source not just of strength but of healing. Faith *can* make us whole.

Over the centuries, the Fathers worked out their detailed understanding of creation on the basis of the thought systems that they knew, largely the philosophical systems of Stoicism and Middle and Late Platonism, which they combined with the science of their day. They found that they had to modify these systems, of course, in order to enable them to accommodate Christ, the incarnate Son of God. But this only had the effect of deepening and expanding the meaning of the concepts they were using.

Today, however, the Church is facing a distinct challenge. Just as the philosophy and science of the ancient world gave no place to Christ until Christians showed how ancient philosophy and science were *completed* by the revelation of the incarnate God, so too today we are surrounded by philosophical and scientific systems which make absolutely no room for God, to say nothing of an *incarnate* God. These thought systems are the norm in our educational establishments and in society as a whole. We are allowed to believe, but not to think of this as anything more than a personal preference. It is not, we are told, a question of Truth. Even the government tells us, in effect: 'Believe what you wish, but don't upset the system.'

The rational conclusion of such a position is that God has nothing to do with the real world, with what *is*, and certainly not with what *should* be. Many, many people would say just this. But the Gospel tells us something different. It tells us that God is so present in the world that simply by turning to him in faith it is possible to be healed. The power of God lies *behind* the world that we see and experience through the senses, and we gain access to it when we turn ourselves towards him and conform ourselves as best we can to his will. Simply by doing what Christ, the Son of God, told them to do the ten lepers were healed. This healing is available to each one of us. It is within us now and available to us – if we will only listen to the commandments of Christ and bring our lives into line with the way of life shown us by him. We can make use of the fact that God *can* heal us from within if we will only listen to what Christ says to us.

One of the tasks facing us as Christians in the twenty-first century is to develop an understanding of the created world that can clarify *why* this should be so. That it *is* so has been shown in the lives of countless men and women.

13

Remembering Paradise

At the beginning of Lent, the Orthodox Church commemorates the expulsion of Adam from Paradise. In effect, we commemorate the Fall and its result: our estrangement from God, and our loss of communion with our Creator. How can this be? How *can* we come to church to recall an event that is the source of all human sadness, of all sorrow, and of all human pain?

We do it because to remember the Fall of Adam is also to remember *whence* he fell: to remember Paradise, to remember where we began, and where God wishes us to return. That memory is precious beyond anything on this earth, for memory is a form of communion, tenuous but real. Our memory, our recollection of someone whom we love – even after many years, even if death itself has intervened – brings with it a presence that makes communion possible. To remember in this way is deeply human, and it lies behind our commemoration of the Fall. Somehow mankind has never forgotten what it was like to live on familiar terms with God. To remember the Fall of Adam, then, is to remember, however faintly, what it was like to be a child of God and to live in this created world as if it were both our Father's house and our own home.

At the Vigil service for the Sunday immediately before the beginning of Lent we hear again and again how Adam lamented his Fall, how he longed to return:[1]

> Adam sat before Paradise, and lamenting his nakedness, he wept:
>
> 'Woe is me! By evil deceit was I persuaded and led astray, and now I am an exile from glory. Woe is me! In my simplicity I was stripped naked and now I am in want. O Paradise, no more shall I take pleasure in thy joy; no more shall I look upon the Lord my God and Maker, for I shall return to the earth whence I was taken ...
>
> In my wretchedness I have cast off the robe woven by God, disobeying thy divine command, O Lord, at the counsel of the enemy; and I am clothed now in fig leaves and in garments of skin. I am condemned to eat the bread of toil in the sweat of my brow, and the earth has been cursed so that it bears thorns and thistles for me ...'

In the course of this lament, from the comments he makes, we learn what life had been like for him in Paradise:

> The Lord my Creator ... honoured me, setting me as ruler upon earth over things visible, and making me a companion of the angels ... O fashioner of the creation and Maker of all, Thou hast taken me from the dust and given me life, commanding me to sing thy praises with thine angels ... Thou hast planted

in Eden the sweetness of Paradise, and bidden me
take my delight in fair and pleasing fruits that
never pass away.

In Eden Adam was even able to see God, and delighted
in the joy and splendour of the godhead. He was clothed
in light (the same robe of light we receive in baptism),
clothed, as it were, in a divinely woven garment, which
is a poetic way of saying that he was filled with the
divine energies of God to such an extent that he radiated
light. The light that shines from eyes and faces of the
saints is but a continuation of that same light.

Nevertheless he says: 'In my wretchedness I have cast
off the robe woven by God, disobeying thy divine command, O Lord, at the counsel of the enemy.' As a result
of his disobedience (Adam himself reminds us in these
hymns that he had transgressed just one commandment
of the Master) he found himself in a world much like the
one we now know. He was cut off from the angels, and
some even appeared hostile to him, guarding the path
back into Eden and preventing his return:

When Adam saw the angel drive him out and shut
the door of the divine garden, he groaned aloud
and said, 'I am fallen, in thy compassion have
mercy on me ... I lament, I groan, I weep as I look
upon the cherubim with the sword of fire set to
guard the gate of Eden against all transgressors.
Woe is me!'

Adam was really naked now, for the glory that had
clothed him was gone. And so he and Eve sewed fig
leaves together and 'made themselves aprons' until God
himself 'made coats of skins' for them 'and clothed
them'. They were now clothed with the skins of mortality, whereas before they had been clothed in im-
mortality and glory. And the earth that had once

produced all that Adam needed now bore thorns and thistles in spite of all his labour.

Adam's Fall affected the whole of creation, since he was himself linked with the whole of creation: 'The sun hid its rays, the moon and the stars were turned to blood, the hills trembled, and the mountains were afraid.' The very leaves of the trees in Paradise shed tears over what had happened, and Adam asks these leaves to pray for him: 'O Paradise', he cries, 'with the sound of thy leaves pray to the Creator that he may not keep thy gate closed for ever.'

Throughout these hymns there is an overpowering sense of *nostalgia*, of longing to return. It is a perception that our present life is a form of exile and that we live now in what can be thought of as a strange and foreign land. Like the Prodigal, in our wilfulness we have left our Father's house, but like him we too have come to our senses, and now long to return. It is because of this that, in the Slav practice, it is customary to sing Psalm 137 (136) during Matins on the last three Sundays before the beginning of Lent. The psalm begins with these words: 'By the rivers of Babylon, there we sat down and there we wept when we remembered Zion ...' It is a lament over the exile of the Jews in Babylon in the sixth century before Christ. A few verses later the Psalmist says: 'If I forget you, O Jerusalem, let my right hand wither! Let my tongue cleave to the roof of my mouth if I do not remember you, if I do not set Jerusalem above my highest joy.' Thus the longing of the Jewish people to return to Jerusalem from exile is likened to our longing to return to Paradise. The linking of this psalm with our commemoration of the expulsion of Adam from Paradise is intended to tell us that we can remember where we have been and that we are not cut off entirely from the world for which we were created.

All of us, in every sphere of our lives – personal, political, or at work – try to shape the world through our own efforts; but by ourselves we are doomed to failure. Without God no good can be done, as it is only by working with God that the world can become transparent to grace. Even as Adam laments for Paradise, he calls on God to save him: 'I cannot enter unless Thou, O Saviour, dost grant me free approach.' What is also required of us at all levels – as individuals, as communities, and as nations – is the desire and the will to be saved. This cannot be inspired by what is small in ourselves, by what is grasping and self-seeking. It must be inspired by what is open and big-hearted in us, by what is capable of including others. And it must also be open to the wisdom – strange and paradoxical – that Christ brought into the world.

This memory of Paradise, then, is important for us. We should build on it and on the longing that accompanies it, in order, to use St Paul's words, to 'put on the armour of light' (Rom 13:12), which to his mind is the equivalent of putting on 'the Lord Jesus Christ'. To 'put on Christ' means to conform our lives to his, the grace for which is given to us in baptism, but fulfilled only through our following the Lord. To follow the Lord, means to follow him through death, through the Cross, and on to Resurrection. This is the path that God has opened for us whereby we may return whence we fell, to Paradise.

14

Our Place in the Cosmos

What does it mean to be human?

A major contribution to Christian anthropology – that is, to the understanding of human beings and our place in the universe – was made by Dionysius the Areopagite, and it is worthwhile to try to see to what extent it can be interpreted in language which is more current than that which he himself used.

Our understanding of Dionysius has had an interesting history. Until the second half of the sixteenth century it was generally accepted that he was the first bishop of Athens, the person mentioned in Acts 17:34 and known to St Paul. The scholars of the Renaissance, however, saw that this could not be true, with the result that an author whose theology had been central to the thought of the Church since the sixth century suddenly became marginal. Participants in the conflicts of the Reformation period used the Fathers largely to bolster their own positions, and a Father who was not what he claimed to be was felt to be a poor support. Luther in particular was critical. In 1520 he declared: 'Dionysius is most pernicious; he Platonises more than he Christianises.' Other Reformers were not so categorical, and some even granted him the status of 'an ancient and learned writer'. Erasmus, for example, seems to have thought that he lived around 300 AD.

Among the Orthodox, however, Dionysius was alive and well. If his work was accepted by other Fathers such as Maximus the Confessor as part of the Orthodox tradition – and indeed as fundamental – then he could retain his place in that tradition even if his dates had to be shifted by five hundred years. Nevertheless, this tradition – and the works it contains – still has to be interpreted and brought to life in each generation.

The Dionysian universe

For Dionysius this world as created by God exists as a great hierarchy of being, clearly distinguished from the world of the divine. The distinction between these two levels of being is so great that if one is said to exist, then the other must be said in some sense not to exist. Being cannot be predicated of both in the same way. If God truly exists, then the created world does not truly exist; but if the created world truly exists, then God does not exist – or at least not in the same way. What is more, while the various levels of created being *participate* in one another, the higher with the lower, the lower with higher, God is 'not participatable' (*amethektos*). There is an ontological gap between creation and Creator at the level of nature, which cannot be bridged at the level of being.

Nevertheless, God is responsible for the existence of the world and imparts to it its being, though in a way which is beyond our understanding. He is also the source and cause of every aspect of created being. As far as we humans are concerned, his *active* presence in the world and in us is mediated through a hierarchy of intermediate beings which Dionysius calls 'angels'. The term is biblical, but the way in which he uses the term is not. These 'angels' exist in layers, one above the other, and they act *in a sense* as mediators between us and God and between God and us. In fact, everything that exists is equally present to God, even if what we encounter in the perceptible world expresses the providential activity of God through these nine ranks of 'angels'. Dionysius makes use of the various biblical names for angels for these nine different ranks This is no coincidence, as the word *angelos* itself in Greek itself means 'messenger', and the angels are, in a sense, 'messengers' between us and God.

Dionysius arranges the nine ranks in groups of three, as in the diagram on p. 138. Other features of the Dionysian world have been added to his scheme: the *nous*, or spiritual intelligence in human beings, and the animal and vegetable souls. At the very bottom is an aspect of creation that Dionysius calls 'soulless and lifeless matter', but which might be thought of as having a 'mechanical' soul. This 'mechanical' soul would be the immediate 'deep structure' of the perceptible world, and the aspect of it to which the physical sciences have access. The Dionysian hierarchy would then look like this.

Although being itself is given directly by God at all levels, all goodness, beauty, life, wisdom and truth, all spiritual strength with the attendant possibility of salvation – all this is conveyed to us via the angels. Without their active participation, we cannot exist, nor can we be saved. Dionysius goes as far as to say that all greatness and smallness, all sameness and difference, all similarity and dissimilarity, all motion and all rest have their source in God. They reach us, however, through the intermediaries of the angelic powers.

Table 1: The Dionysian World

GOD

- - - -

(((Seraphim)))
((((Cherubim))))
(((((Thrones)))))

- - - - - - - - - - - -

(((((Powers)))))))
(((((Dominions)))))
((((((Authorities))))))

— - - - - - - - - - : - - -

(((((Principalities)))))
(((((((Archangels)))))))
((((((((((Angels))))))))))

—- - - - - - - - - - - - - - -

(((((((Nous)))))))

- - - - - - - - - - - - -

((((((Animal Soul))))))
(((((((Vegetable Soul)))))))
((((((((((Mechanical Soul))))))))))

- - - - - - - - - - - - - - - - - -

Perceptible World

What then is the nature of the 'angels'? To begin with, one order is not like the next. They are structured in the sense that while the higher order can 'comprehend' the lower, the lower cannot 'comprehend' the higher. They are also structured in the sense that the unity, and integration, of a higher order is always greater than that of the one below it: diversity increases as one progresses down the hierarchy of angelic forms and decreases as one moves upward. As a result, the higher can impart unity to the lower, but the lower cannot impart unity to the higher. In the end, of course, only God is one, and it is he who ultimately underpins the unity of the whole of creation. This scheme is not without its biblical and liturgical foundation: the vision of Isaiah 6 does not indicate how many seraphim the prophet saw, but the implication is that the number was not large. At the other end of the scale, the other hand, reference is made in the Liturgy of St John Chrysostom to 'thousands of archangels' who are followed by 'tens of thousands of angels'.[1] We should imagine that the complexity of the various orders of angels increases with their number as they are found to be further and further from God.

In philosophical terms, this means that the angelic hierarchies can be thought of as a series of 'meta-languages', each of which is able to comprehend and give meaning to the 'language' of the order immediately below it, but is unable to comprehend fully anything that is higher. One is reminded here of Goedel's Theorem, which states that in any mathematical system complex enough to provide for simple arithmetic, true statements can be formulated which can nevertheless not be proved to be true within that system. In other words, *all* systems of thought are destined to be in-complete. To comprehend completely any verbalised and rational system, a second, higher system must be used. Something similar seems to be going on in Dionysius when he says that each angelic order is able to comprehend the order below it, but not the order above.

Approaching the Dionysian system from another point of view, each angelic layer can be thought of as a field of force, distinct from the rank above and from the rank below, internally consistent and one with itself, yet capable of influencing and determining the scope of activity of the field below it, but not the field above. The notion of participation, of course, implies that the lower field is in a position to influence to some extent the field above, but not to alter its fundamental nature, much as gravity is able to influence the movement of light. Like all fields of force, the angelic powers become perceptible only through their effect on the perceptible world, though in the realm of the noumenal there will be noumenal and imperceptible effects.[2]

The Dionysian world might seem to be terribly constricting, with each order of angel controlling the order below it, and this would certainly be the case were it not for human freedom. What about the role of chance, however, in the Dionysian scheme? It would appear that at an atomic and subatomic level the so-called 'material' world includes phenomena that cannot be shown to take place as the result of any particular cause. They just happen. Is there any place for such phenomena in the Dionysian hierarchy?

Here, again, we shall have to do Dionysius' work for him. If we imagine, as Dionysius tells us, that the unity and integration of the successive layers of angelic powers increases as they come nearer and nearer to God, then we are entitled to ask what happens if we move in the opposite direction and down the hierarchy. It would appear that what might be called a 'loss of control' can only arise in the very lowest level, at the level of the 'mechanical' soul that is studied by chemistry and physics. The 'mechanical soul' that is reflected in the laws of physics does not determine completely the behaviour of all the particles that are present in the universe. It tells us what is likely to happen to them from a statistical point of view, but not what will happen in detail.

It is as if the various orders of the hierarchy were somehow revolving around God (as Dionysius says they do) and as they get further and further away from the centre the forces that bind them together get weaker and weaker, until at a certain stage the very lowest of the orders, the 'mechanical soul', loses control, and phenomena begin to appear whose appearance cannot be predicted. It would be something like what happens on a galactic scale, where matter at the very edge of the galaxy seems to be thrown off into space and escape the control of the galaxy as a whole. The *logos* of the 'mechanical soul' would still determine the behaviour of the perceptible world in the ordinary world in which we live, but the behaviour of this world at the level of atomic and subatomic particles could only be described statistically.

It is quite clear, however, that if we are to imagine that this is taking place in the three-dimensional space in which we live, then all these fields will have to co-exist within the same coordinates. They will lie on top of one another and within one another. There is nothing strange about this, since we know that this happens all the time even in the world that the physical sciences reveal to us. The various forms of energy, such as gravity, electromagnetic energy, light, and the strong and weak atomic binding forces – all these 'overlap', and the presence of one does not prevent the presence of the other. The point to be grasped is that the Dionysian world is at least as complex as the world to which we have access through modern science.

To be convinced of the extraordinary nature of the world as we now understand it, we have only to perform a simple thought experiment. Imagine that we are able to transport ourselves into space and can take with us a huge telescope capable of rotating in all directions and picking up signals from the farthest edges of the universe. (This has already been realised in part, of course, in the Hubble telescope.) We can easily understand that light from the most distant perceptible galaxies in the universe is reaching the spot at which we are. Not only

is this true, however, but if we were to remove the telescope entirely, we can see that these light waves, coming
from every direction, would all, in theory, be passing
through a single point. At every point in outer space,
therefore, there is in theory information of unimaginable
complexity available in the form of light waves, radio
waves and other radiation concerning every point on
the circumference of the known universe. These waves
do not, apparently, interfere seriously with one another,
and maintain their imperceptibility until a device is
introduced that renders them accessible to the human
eye. The notion that fields of force and waves of various
kinds can occupy the same three-dimensional space has
now been with us a long time.

Applying this picture to the Dionysian world, we
would need to say that each angelic layer, each of these
hierarchically arranged 'fields of force', is able to integrate and unify the layer below it while preserving its
own internal harmony. At the same time it contains a
level of unity, or oneness, that is greater than that of the
order below it, a unity that the lower order is unable
'grasp' or 'comprehend'.

The position of mankind

Everything thus far has concerned the upper part of the
diagram given above. Human beings are found in the
lower portion. For Dionysius, the angelic world, the
world of rational (*logikoi*) beings, is complemented by a
world of 'souls'. In a very important passage in the
Divine Names Dionysius distinguishes three layers of
non-angelic being: the animal realm, the vegetable realm
and the inanimate realm.[3] He lists them in hierarchical
order, just as he lists the various orders of angels, and it
is consistent with his thought to range them in order at
the bottom of our diagram. The first two orders are said

to possess 'souls', while the lowest is apparently without a soul, though I have taken the liberty of giving it a 'mechanical soul' to reflect what we know about its activity. Each layer of being – except, of course, the last – is capable of ordering and giving unity to the level below it. Each exists at a level of integration that is greater than the level below. Each somehow includes the level below it and raises it towards the oneness of God.

In other words, there are aspects of vegetable life that can be treated as inanimate (such as the chemical fertilisers that we spread on our fields), just as there are aspects of animal life that can be treated as if they were of a vegetable nature (one thinks of what goes on in the intestines of a human being, a process not entirely unlike what goes on in a compost pile) – but the vegetable soul integrates the inanimate world at a higher level than it would otherwise possess, while the animal soul integrates the vegetable world at a higher level as well.

The human being, however, is not just an animal. Humans are endowed with *nous*, the spiritual intellect, which integrates their animal being at yet a higher level and links with the angelic world. In fact, in Dionysius the angelic orders are called *noes*, which is simply the plural form of *nous*. Through the *nous* mankind is put in touch with higher spheres of creation, and is said to share with them the characteristic of being 'rational' (*logikos*).

The picture of creation presented, when all these elements are integrated in it, is of an inanimate world, part of which is integrated at the level of vegetable life through the vegetable soul, while a portion of this level of the creation is further integrated at a higher level through the presence of the animal soul. Then finally, a small part of the animal world is given an even higher level of integration and drawn even nearer to God and his oneness by the *nous* that is found in every human being. This process can be conceived of as continuing through the angelic orders, with each higher order exhibiting greater integration and oneness, until finally the seraphim stand in immediate proximity to God, around whom they constantly circle and sing. Once again, we must remember that although we have been using the language of 'up' and 'down', as does Dionysius, the language that is appropriate for the description of our three-dimensional world is actually inappropriate here. All these levels of beings exist simultaneously on top of one another, coinciding without confusion, just as the light waves in space exist on top of one another without confusion. The language of 'up' and 'down' is a metaphor, and we must recognise its limitations.

The nature of the material world

Dionysius is not very interested in the animal, vegetable or inanimate worlds. In fact, he is not very interested in 'matter' at all, except in so far as the material world provides him with images that help him convey what he understands to be happening in the noumenal realm. The material world is the 'phenomenal' or 'perceptible' world. It is *defined* by being perceptible, not by having mass (i.e., consisting of a quantity of 'matter'). In the Dionysian world, 'mass' is best understood as our perception of the resistance that one field of force offers to another, i.e. phenomenologically.

In what sense, then, does the perceptible exist, and what is its relationship to the world of 'souls' (*psykhai*) and 'intelligences' (*noes*)? Unfortunately, Dionysius does not discuss this question, so we will have to do his work for him. The simplest way to understand this relationship is to accept that the perceptible world is the phenomenal aspect of the 'deep structure' of the inanimate realm, that is mediated to that realm by the higher levels of the Dionysian hierarchy. If we follow Maximus the Confessor and take it as given that each level of being has the ability to perceive and to be perceived at its own level, but that it can neither be truly grasped for what it is by what is 'below' it nor truly grasp that which is 'above' it, then in some sense the lowest order of being is most simply defined as that which can perceive and be perceived by the senses. It is to this order that, in their 'mechanical' aspect, our senses belong. Plants will be able to 'perceive' this realm, but will not be able to be perceived by it as plants, only as inanimate beings. Animals in turn will perceive one another as such, and will perceive plants as plants. They will not be able to perceive human beings, however, as other than as animals of another kind.

Human beings, however, who are endowed with *nous*, the 'spiritual intellect', will not only be able to perceive other humans as creatures like themselves, but will be able to perceive and distinguish the animal, vegetable and inanimate realms that are positioned below us. They will have only a partial understanding, however, of the noumenal realm of angelic powers that lie above them and will tend to think of them as human beings – which is how they are normally depicted in literature and art.

It is important to stress the *bound* nature of the relations between the different orders of the Dionysian hierarchy. Thus far we have seen no indication that there is movement between the orders. There is no change of position. What each order can or cannot understand, what it can or cannot do is strictly determined by its position in the hierarchy. This, of course, raises a serious problem: how can a human being have any immediate knowledge of God since he or she is separated from God by so many intervening orders of angels? These intervening orders should in theory act as a screen and impede true knowledge of God. This issue is bound up with the nature of the person.

The Fall

Dionysius has very little to say about the Fall, just as he has little to say about human freedom. On the basis of the diagram given above, however, it is clear that the Fall will have involved not only the human being with his *nous*, but also those aspects of the animal, vegetable and inanimate realm with which he is directly involved, that part of creation which it is now our task to reposition under the sovereignty of God. Because of the participation of the *nous* in the level of being that lies above it, however, the Fall will also have affected at least the lowest order of angels. It could conceivably have affected the higher orders as well. If we think of the various orders as being fields of force, structured forms of energy bearing with them all the qualities of the world, then each will affect to a certain extent both the level above and that below. Thus the Fall will have affected both human beings and angels if its starting point was human, or human beings, the angels *and* the archangels if its starting point was at an angelic level.

In any case, the Fall will have involved only a *distortion* of being. For Dionysius evil is not something that exists in its own right. It is ultimately parasitic in nature. For evil to come into being requires a pre-existing aspect of God's good creation that can become distorted by turning from the path proposed for it by God. This rift in creation can only be introduced by freedom. Human freedom implies that human beings, the lower angelic powers, and those aspects of creation that these two types of being can affect, are able to live and act in a manner that is foreign to the deep structure of creation as intended by the Creator. The 'foundations of the earth' are not shaken, of course, for human freedom cannot overthrow the deep structure of the world as created and sustained by the almighty power of God. Nevertheless, on earth God's will is not being carried out. It is being carried out, however, everywhere else in the universe.

The person

Dionysius does not spend much time discussing the notion of the person, but certain things can nevertheless be said about the place of the person in his scheme. To begin with, it is clear that the Incarnation, in which the Son and Word of God takes on flesh, will involve the Word's involvement with all the angelic and lower orders of being. In order to be fully human, the incarnate Word will also need to possess *nous*. To appear in the perceptible world the Word must 'descend' from his position 'outside' and 'above' creation and be present even in the lowest levels of being. To use the language of some of the Fathers, the Word must become 'thick'. By doing so the Word, of course, unites all levels of creation to himself. This follows from the manner in which even the perceptible realm participates, at least indirectly, in all the higher levels of being. Without this participation, the world of perception could not exist, nor would it be able to reflect the providential concern and activity of God.

The mode of relationship with creation into which the eternal Word enters, however, is not a 'natural' one, since there is no this-worldly or 'natural' relationship between God and creation. It is *hypostatic* – personal – in character, and depends ultimately only upon the free and personal will of God. It is therefore a freely assumed relationship, and completely personal in nature. It is made possible only by the way the whole of creation is *hypostatically* related to the Creator from the moment of creation. This is extremely important for our understanding of our place of in the Dionysian scheme. The *hypostatic* reality that is the second Person of the Trinity is able to assume a personal relationship with all that exists in a way that preserves our human freedom within the natural world. The relationship of the Word to creation is 'kenotic' in that after his Incarnation the Son retains the freedom he had before, but within the limitations that accompany human existence. The *hypostatic* relationship of the Word with creation existed 'from the beginning' through the act of creation itself, but it has been given the greatest possible depth and immediacy through the Incarnation.

The human hypostasis or person is also not a 'natural' reality. The human being, as person, somehow transcends nature and does not have the limitations that constrict the life and being of all other creatures. In the Dionysian scheme, the higher is able to 'comprehend' the lower, but the lower is unable to 'comprehend' the higher. Yet the human person is somehow able to 'comprehend' the whole. It is possible for a human being to have 'the mind of Christ' and perceive the meaning of the whole of God's creation.

Dionysius was aware of this problem, though he does not address it directly. In chapter 13 of the *Celestial Hierarchies* he attempts to answer the question of why the prophet Isaiah is said to have been purified by the seraphim (cf. Isa 6:7). He offers two answers. The first, introduced by the expression 'some would say this', accepts that all he has said about the relation of the successive angelic orders to each other would seem to indicate that the seraphim could not possibly have descended to the level of Isaiah, a prophet but still only a human being, and that therefore the task of purifying him must have been transmitted downwards through the heavenly orders until it reached an 'angel', a member of the lowest order, who carried out the purification. This angel is called a 'seraph' in Scripture because the process was carried out by means of fire. This is a picture of mankind locked into the world of nature and devoid of the *hypostatic*, personal existence that would enable mankind to understand the whole. The order of angels appears here as a kind of ceiling above which we cannot penetrate.

Dionysius goes on to say, however, that 'someone else has provided me with an answer to this problem which is not completely inappropriate'. According to this individual, whose identity we never learn, the angel who initiated the prophet

> fashioned this vision [*orasis*] for the purpose of instructing the prophet [i.e., Isaiah] in divine matters ... For he who said this said that the Divine First Power goes forth visiting all things, and irresistibly penetrates all things, and yet is invisible to all ... [It] bestows the radiance of Its Light upon the most exalted beings through whom, as leaders, It is imparted to the lower choirs in order according to their power of divine contemplation.[4]

This angel then 'referred his own office of purification first to God, and after God to that first Hierarchy'. In this picture the prophet does actually see the seraphim, but only according to his own capacity:

> He who gave this explanation used to say that the vision was shown to the prophet by one of those holy and blessed Angels who preside over us, by whose enlightening guidance he was raised to that intellectual contemplation in which he beheld the

most exalted Beings (to speak in symbols) established under God, with God and around God; and their super-princely Leader [i.e. the eternal Word of God], ineffably uplifted above them all, established in the midst of the supremely exalted Powers.[5]

In this model the prophet is the recipient of a vision provided by the 'mighty angel' in charge of his purification, a vision that comes to him by virtue of the mediating ranks of heavenly powers. It is a mediated vision of God and the seraphim, appropriate to the capacity of the receiver, and enables the seer to relate directly, though imperfectly, to God and the highest powers. Here we seem to have a description of true *hypostatic* existence which is in touch with all levels of being and is similar, to this extent, to the hypostatic existence of the Incarnate Christ. The human being – in this case, Isaiah – is able to relate as *person* to the whole of creation and not just to the realms below him. He is able, in theory, to grasp the whole of its structure and the whole of its meaning.

15

Dionysius and the
Scientific Enterprise

As we can see, it is very difficult for contemporary Christians to translate their understanding of what it is to be human into a language that is capable of reaching ordinary people. These 'ordinary' people may be individuals with no great educational or cultural background, they may be highly cultured people with a broad understanding of history and literature, or they may simply be people who are imbued with the prevailing positivistic, 'scientific' understanding that is spread through our schools, newspapers and much popular literature. Nevertheless, this work of translation is an important task of theology, and one that we shall have to undertake if we are reach not only our fellow Christians, but also those who have yet to come to know Christ as the Church knows him.

Thus far Dionysius has been presented largely in his

own terms, using his language and not leaving the cultural and spiritual world of which he was a part except to seek occasional analogies in the world opened to us by modern science. What would happen, however, if we were to confront his picture of reality with that which is in general use today? The scientific enterprise of the past few centuries is one of the great success stories of the human intellect or *nous*. An approach to the perceptible world has been developed that has enabled us to grasp fairly accurately the 'deep structure' of its existence behind the veil of perceptible phenomena. Even though this deep structure can never be seen directly, the application of mathematics in an extremely imaginative way has given us a relatively clear picture of what is going on in the noumenal, imperceptible realm. We would not have been able to put a man on the moon if our theories about the hidden structure of the perceptible world were very wrong.

What happens, then, if we confront the Dionysian world with the world of modern science? The first thing we should note is that the physical sciences are a systematic, shared human investigation of the noumenal, imperceptible, aspect of the perceptible realm. What has become clear during the past four centuries is that this noumenal aspect to which we have access through science is to a great extent mathematical in nature. Behind the perceptible world there lies a world of mathematically describable forms that are the structure on which our perceptions of colour, sound, smell, taste and touch are hung. It also seems clear that there is nothing that we perceive that does not have a noumenal, mathematically describable substrate that we as humans have the ability to conceive.

This substrate can be described in terms of energy and form: neither ever occurs without the other.

Nevertheless, the actual perceptions we enjoy cannot be described in terms of energy and form. They bring something else with them that is a 'plus' over and beyond the 'scientific', mathematical description of their causal agencies. The colour red is not expressible in three dimensions, even if the periodicity of the wave of light that lies behind it is. The smell of burnt toast does not belong to realm of the measurable, even if the shapes of the various molecules that produce the sensation in us are. The reasons why we can distinguish different smells, that is, the mathematical structure of the molecules that make up our organs of taste perception and the shapes of the molecules that bring taste with them, will no doubt some day be described in detail, but the taste of a rotten egg is not three-dimensional. The length and intensity of the sound waves that convey to us the melody of a Mozart aria can even be rendered visible, but the sound itself does not have shape or structure except in a metaphorical sense. Similarly, the resistance that I experience as pressure when I lean against a wall can in theory be completely described in mathematical terms, in terms or energy and form, but my perception of the pressure itself is not a three-dimensional reality, any more than is the pain I feel when I cut my finger.

In the Dionysian world (and for Maximus the Confessor) these 'pluses', these perceptions that exist over and above the mathematical reality that lies behind their presence, have their origin in God, as does everything that is. They too are transmitted to us by the hierarchy of 'souls' and 'intellects' that has been created by God and structures the whole of creation. God is the ultimate source of all that is. In the oneness of God, which includes the divine Logos, there exists all the diversity of the world.

The three-dimensional, mathematically analysable and noumenal substrate that underlies the world of our perceptions (and is the immediate object of the scientific enterprise) involves only the three-dimensional, inanimate, mechanical level of the Dionysian world. All other levels, from the vegetable soul up through the animal soul, the *nous* and the subsequent angelic orders are non-spatial in character, or at least cannot be described in three dimensions. It may in theory be possible to describe aspects of their being in mathematical terms, but this description will not be formulated in conventional, Euclidean terms. What is more, these higher levels exist alongside and within the inanimate realm that is the primary object of scientific investigation. At every point they form an imperceptible ladder *between* – if this is the right word – the perceptible realm and God.

Against this Dionysian background we are in a position to say that certain scientific disciplines address themselves to certain levels of the hierarchy of being. On the basis of the diagram in the previous chapter, it is clear that the physical sciences concern themselves with the immediate noumenal and mathematically structured substrate of perceptible being. Biology then deals with the somewhat more complicated 'vegetable soul' and the creatures it integrates, while zoology is concerned with those beings that are integrated by the 'animal soul'. Anthropology and the human sciences are focused on the human being, whose existence is, by nature, shaped and integrated by the *nous*, the 'spiritual intellect' that is the peculiar attribute of mankind.

The vision of creation set out by Dionysius the Areopagite in the first part of the sixth century is capable, then, of providing a framework within which the various sciences can fit quite comfortably and where

they can do their work. This is true because for
Dionysius the universe has depth, and the different
sciences address reality at varying levels of complexity.
Even the simplest atomic or sub-atomic particle will be
connected with its Creator by a ladder of intermediate
forms, forms that are filled with energy and are active in
sustaining creation. The physical sciences study the
deep structure of the lowest and simplest of these forms,
while biology, zoology and anthropology address the
higher, more complicated levels of existence. Only at the
lowest perceptible level will Euclidean geometry be of
any use. At any higher level, until we develop a method-
ology that will enable us to get behind the Euclidean
world, we are reduced to using metaphors or statistical
methods to describe what we see. Though it is possible
to provide a mathematical analysis of plant life and its
processes at the level of its inanimate reality, something
that is of real use in a practical sense, no merely mathematical formula will ever get to the heart of plant life as
it gets to the heart of a chemical reaction. The same can
be said and with greater justification when we consider
animal life and finally human life.

When it comes to the angels, moreover, Dionysius is
quite correct when he says that by and large we are
reduced to describing them in images taken from the
perceptible world. No mathematical models have yet
been developed that will allow us to describe these
higher-order and probably non-linear fields and wave
functions in such a way as to enable us to conceptualise
in mathematical terms their action on the fields and
functions that we find behind our three-dimensional
world. The day may come, of course, but we are still
waiting.[1]

In the meantime we should not hesitate to make use
of the world view of Fathers such as Dionysius the

Areopagite. There is much more in their 'philosophy' than is dreamed of in the philosophy that is contained in the 'scientific' world view now communicated so widely in our schools and universities. One of the Fathers has been used here to illustrate this point, but others could just as easily have been used. In fact, we should begin to analyse the thought of the Fathers systematically, with a view to seeing which of their approaches provides the best framework for the understanding of the scientific enterprise of the past three centuries. The scientific enterprise is the greatest and most sustained intellectual effort yet produced by human beings, and we must be ready to find a place for it in our thought as Christians. If we do not, we run the risk of losing our ability to provide people with the tools they need to understand and embrace the world in which they live.

16

An 'Ecology of the Virtues': the Ecological Crisis and the Objectification of Nature

What we are facing now on a worldwide scale is not a technological crisis; it is not a political crisis; it is not an economic crisis; nor is it even fundamentally an ecological crisis. Neither is it the result of getting a few things wrong. We are in crisis because we have created, as the background to our decisions, a thought world in which the inner world of humanity has no place. We should not be surprised, therefore, if the world our actions then produce turns out to be somehow inhuman, and inimical to our very survival. There is no question but that the human race today has a huge problem about its relationship to creation. Nobody doubts for a moment that we are on course to destroy the habitat in which we live. If our decisions are taken against the background of a view of the universe from which our inner world has been removed, we can hardly be surprised when the results of our choices do not serve us well. What starts from inhuman premises will end with inhuman results.

Various forms of 'godlessness' have risen to the surface on a massive scale in recent centuries, enabling leaders to take decisions in the name of humanity that were profoundly inimical to humanity. As we look back over the French Revolution, Nazi Germany, Soviet Russia, the 'Cultural Revolution' in China, the 'Killing Fields' of Cambodia, to say nothing of more recent events, it becomes harder and harder to think of them as aberrations. From the point of view of the objective historian, these phenomena differ considerably in the way they developed over time; but there is nonetheless an inner coherence that we now can see, looking back, in a way that was not possible – for most people – at the time.

In our present world, we are constantly being told to seek the most efficient way to do things, in business, in government, in the health service, in education. To be efficient, of course, can only be a good thing. It means to increase profits, to reduce taxation, to improve services. Surely these are all good things. But we need to ask ourselves: what lies behind this drive for efficiency? How should it be assessed from a theological point of view, from the point of view of the Gospel? Is it inspired by anything more than greed, lust for power, a desire for physical comfort – and the fear of death?

The objectification of nature, and self-erasure from creation

The scientific view of the world does concern itself with 'truth', but this truth is essentially of a mathematical nature. Already in the thirteenth century Roger Bacon declared that 'Mathematics is the gate and key of the sciences,' by which he meant the gateway and key to the understanding of Nature, which is God's creation.

In the course of the gradual development of the scientific world view, however, there has come about an 'objectification' of our relationship to the world. The observer is removed from the accepted picture of the natural order. Nature exists 'out there', independently of ourselves. It is a non-personal 'other' on which we can carry out mental and physical operations, which we can mentally and physically dissect. Paradoxically, this is true even though developments over the past century in the field of physics make it quite clear that at the atomic and sub-atomic level, the observer, through the instruments that he uses to investigate the behaviour of the physical world, modifies that world and influences his observations. In other words, the observer himself is part of the picture and must be understood as such. In fact, it is not clear that a world, a 'cosmos', can exist as we understand it without an observer – though the potential for existence is always there. The word 'exist' has as its Latin root *exsistere*, meaning 'to stand forth, to come forth, to emerge, to appear'. Only in the presence of the observer does the world 'exist' in this etymological sense; only in the presence of an observer does it 'come into being', 'emerge (into existence)'.

What is marvellous about human beings, of course, is that we *can* look at ourselves from outside and put ourselves into the picture. To be able to look at oneself, to have a certain 'distance' from oneself, is of course the miracle of *self*-consciousness, the extraordinary ability of human beings to put distance between ourselves and the contents of our own minds. This is a capacity of the *nous*, and is at the very heart of our hypostatic existence and the spiritual life. It is also what will enable us to put ourselves back into the picture we have of nature, and thereby cease editing ourselves out of creation.

The world of physics: reducing the real to the mathematical

This form of 'self-erasure' has been helped by a second development that has taken place over the last few centuries, though its origins go far back into the Ancient World. When, as rational, scientific beings, we think about the real world, we think of it as being made up of a kind of 'substance' that has no qualities. This notion is counter-intuitive in terms of the world of naïve realism in which we normally live: the world in which we move is filled with colours, sounds, smells and things to taste. Just watch a nine-month old child exploring everything in sight by putting it into his or her mouth.

All this is edited out of the world that our physics textbooks describe. What remains is substance without attributes, the Cartesian world of mathematically conceived 'extension' in which 'real qualities' do not exist, while the 'qualified' world ends up as a feature only of our inner world, the non-spatial, incorporeal mind, which, for Descartes, was located in the pineal gland behind the brain. Not only is beauty 'in the eye of the beholder', but all colour, taste, smell, sound and tactile sensation is also 'in the eye of the beholder'. The 'real' world of physics is somehow without all these. It has its own striking beauty, of course, but it is the beauty of mathematics, just as the game of chess has its own beauty and fascination – and for some it can become a whole world.

This desire to reduce the real to the mathematical goes back to Ancient Greeks, and its origin can be traced to their earliest attempts to understand nature. The rationalisation of nature is the driving force behind the thought of the Ionian philosophers such a Thales, Anaxagoras and Heraclitus, each of whom identified one substance that maintained its identity behind the changes of the perceptible world. For the Pythagoreans, however, 'All things are numbers': number was declared to be at the heart of all that exists. In the words of Philolaos, a famous fifth-century member of the school, 'Were it not for number and its nature, nothing that exists would be clear to anybody either in itself or in its relation to other things ...' This belief was underpinned by their investigation of music and the movement of the heavenly bodies and by the rapid progress made by the Greeks in geometry and arithmetic. Already in *Philebus*, Plato had expressed the thought that each science is only truly a science to the extent that it contains mathematics. The Greeks, in a brilliant fashion, were able to show clearly and convincingly that the world we live in is structured along mathematical lines.

At the same time, Plato also gave expression to another fundamental idea of the classical world view: the eternal nature of matter. In the *Timaeus* Plato develops his notion of a 'demiurge' who fashions the world we see on the basis of an ideal world which is also eternal. This 'workman' god does not therefore create the universe out of nothing, *ex nihilo*, but works on pre-existing 'stuff'. As a result, of course, the world is not contingent, entirely dependent upon a Creator for its existence, as in the Jewish, Christian and Islamic traditions, but a self-standing reality.

This belief in a world formed from an unqualified substance and defined mathematically, underpinned the classical understanding of the material world. As time went on many different theories were developed, some of which backed off from the thoroughgoing rationalisation of nature found among the Pythagoreans. Among these, of course, was Aristotle, for whom mathematical constructs were incapable of embracing qualitative differences such a colour and smell. As abstractions from experience, they are not independent of or prior to experience. They exist in our minds as ideas mediating between the object and the essence of the object. Strange as it may seem, the gradual rejection during the fifteenth and sixteenth centuries of the Aristotelian physics that had come to dominate Western thinking in the twelfth and thirteenth centuries, actually marked a return to the mathematically based model of classical Greek physics. This in turn, of course, made possible the discoveries of Kepler, Galileo and Newton.

In our own age, a view of the world that was the province of the educated few in the Ancient World has become the possession of the many. We are taught a 'scientific' view of the material world in which the most penetrating form of scientific exploration – physics – is also the field least connected with the world as experienced in ordinary life. In a way, we seem to have fallen in love with the notion of 'unqualified' substance, substance without colour or taste or smell. The 'accidents' of matter exist only in our minds. They do not belong to the real world, the three-dimensional world of spatial extension. They don't really 'exist' in that etymological sense of naturally 'emerging from' the world that the physical sciences describe for us.

Maximus the Confessor: a quality-filled world

Maximus the Confessor, however, stresses the God-givenness of the qualified world, the world as perceived by the senses. All that we see or perceive in any manner is an expression of the will of God, because even 'qualified substances' express the *logos* of their inner nature.

The colours of a sunset, the shape of a tree's leaves, all the varieties of fish that one can find in the sea – all smells and all tastes – each and every one of them is an expression of God's will for creation. The beauty of the world in all its diversity can be thought of as a gift to us – and therefore *through* the world we are enabled to relate to God the Creator of all that is.

As we have already seen, Maximus distinguishes between the 'principle' or *logos* of a created nature, its *logos physeôs*, which pre-exists in the *Logos* of God, and its 'mode of being' or *tropos hyparkseôs*. In this three-dimensional world outside ourselves, God's providential care is at work and it is there that the *Logos* of God is busy, preserving both qualitative difference and qualitative interrelation through the 'mode of being' of individual entities. Throughout almost all of creation the 'principle of nature' and 'mode of being' of each entity are the same, though perhaps it would be better to say that each entity's 'mode of being' *expresses* the 'principle' of its nature. In creatures endowed with freedom, however (those which are *autokinêtoi*, such as human beings), these two need not coincide. A discrepancy can arise, and the actual movement and development of such a creature can differ from the plan originally envisaged for it by God.

In the world of Maximus experience is given real weight – and ultimately divine significance. It is also a world in which we should feel at home, not only because the qualified entities among which we live have a God-given a place in it, but also because the involvement in them of the eternal Logos of God somehow calls for our close and attentive examination. It is also a world in which the *way* in which we live – or should live – must be the focus of our attention. The way in which Maximus integrates human behaviour into his cosmology is deeply significant for us today.

If, by contrast, we look at the development of the current scientific paradigm, we find it structured by the attitudes of two very important thinkers, Francis Bacon (1561–1626) and René Descartes (1596–1650). Bacon proposed the mastery of nature, rather than an understanding of the purposes God had built into the natural world, as the goal of scientific investigation. He wished to 'command nature for the service and welfare of man, not to please and delight scholars'. As he saw it, science could 'provide man with "infinite commodities", endow human life with inventions and riches, and minister to the conveniences and comforts of man'. Such are 'the true and lawful goals of science'.[1] These same attitudes found expression a few years later in the work of Descartes, who says that by studying natural phenomena and understanding them 'as distinctly as we know the different crafts of our artisans, we can in the same way employ them in all those uses to which they are adapted, and thus render ourselves the masters and possessors of nature'.[2]

Descartes was a brilliant mathematician. His work on coordinate geometry and its relationship to algebra laid the foundations for the development of the calculus and all subsequent mathematics. In a departure from the attitude taken in the Ancient World, he believed algebra to be superior to geometry through its universality and the way in which it managed to 'mechanise' the reasoning process and thereby minimise the work involved in solving problems. It was more 'efficient' than geometry, which is so tied to figures that, as he said, 'it can exercise the understanding only on condition of greatly fatiguing the imagination'.[3] What is striking is that Descartes seems to have cared little for the beauty and harmony of mathematics. Mathematics is not for him a contemplative discipline, but a constructive and useful science. Mathematical method applied only to mathematics is without value because it is not a study of nature, and 'those who cultivate mathematics for its own sake are idle searchers given to the vain play of the spirit'.[4]

Both Bacon and Descartes, of course, were believers. Nevertheless, the elimination of 'final causes' and the rationalisation and mathematicisation of nature opened the way for the thinkers of the following century, who were often openly hostile to Christianity and to all 'supernatural' religion. Reason now reigned supreme and happiness in this life was felt to be the appropriate goal of all human endeavour. A side effect of this tendency was an easy optimism and a general insensitivity to the existence of sin. 'Life, liberty and the pursuit of happiness' became the goal of the political process – and of human activity in general. 'Life' in this context means *this* life, of course; 'liberty' means the right to do what one wants so long as it does not interfere with the rights of others; 'the pursuit of happiness' means largely the pursuit of those 'commodities', 'conveniences', 'comforts' and 'riches' of which Francis Bacon speaks, using the power over nature that Descartes thought was the proper goal of human intellectual activity.

All of this is very familiar. These ideas are very near to being the 'civic religion' of the most powerful nation the world has ever known and sometimes seem close to becoming the civic religion of the United Kingdom as well. But whether they form an adequate foundation for human life – to say nothing of the Christian life – requires investigation.

From the point of view of Maximus, however, things look very different. Not only is the world of nature created by God a world of 'qualified substances', so that it will never be possible to understand it in purely mathematical terms, but it also has an end, a goal, built into its deep structure from the beginning. This is the object of the 'natural contemplation' – or, perhaps, better, 'contemplation of nature' (*physikê theôria*) – of which the ascetic tradition speaks. To understand the world in depth, it is necessary to understand what God intends it to be. Any other understanding touches only the surface of reality. For Maximus, of course, and indeed for the Church itself in the early centuries, the *ultimate* goal of mankind – and therefore of the universe – is deification, *theôsis*.

The crisis we are facing today, however, takes place at a much lower level. We need to find out how we can live in relationship to the earth in such a way as to prevent the gradual deterioration of our surroundings to a point where life – at least human life – is no longer possible. When we address the ecological situation, we are addressing our own survival.

It is impossible to go into the detail of the historical cultural processes that have led us to our present situation. Nor is there any need, for we know them – from within. We are *all* implicated in our present situation, whether we are aware of it or not. And here perhaps we need to allow for the notion of 'unwitting' sin. In the Orthodox prayers for the dead, we ask God to forgive the person who has departed this life 'all his sins, both voluntary and involuntary'. Why? Because even involuntary sin separates us from God, and it is that separation that we hope will be overcome by God in his mercy – if necessary, after death.

It is the gift of freedom, itself bound up with the image of God in human beings, that made sin possible, since it made possible a discrepancy *within* the created world between what God wills and that which is. In Maximus's understanding of the spiritual life this discrepancy is the result of self-love (*philautia*), which encapsulates all other forms of sin. *Philautia* is the opposite of *philanthrôpia*, 'love for mankind', the overriding characteristic of God, which is mentioned again and again in the prayers of the Eastern Church. The 'tear' or 'rent' which sin has introduced into the fabric of creation can be repaired only by imitation of God, more specifically by imitation of Christ, who is himself the revelation of God's love for mankind and tells us that he does only what he see the Father do. It is through *philanthrôpia* that we restore our relationship with our neighbour, and in doing so restore our relationship with God, fulfilling the double commandment on which 'hang all the law and the prophets' (Mt 22:40).

Gratitude, thankfulness (*eukharistia*) for God's *philanthrôpia* can be shown to him in two ways: first, by turning to God in love; and second, by passing on God's love for us by turning it outwards towards others, to our neighbours, in the form of our own love for mankind. In this way we both imitate God, becoming 'God-like', and fulfil the double commandment given by Christ. Self-love, *philautia*, is an expression of our refusal to accept the double commandment to love both God and our neighbour. It leads first to the *dis*integration of the individual, in that the soul of the person who is given over to self-love is no longer is related properly to his or her body. In such a person the soul obeys the body and is governed from below, rather than controlling and commanding the body, as it should. At the same time it does not relate properly to the *nous*, the spiritual intelligence, since it is in revolt against the higher understanding of life that the *nous* is capable of providing.

This *dis*integration of an individual leads inevitably to the *dis*integration of humanity as a whole, of the 'one man' that has existed since the creation of Adam. Like

Eve, we were all taken from Adam and are 'bone of his bone and flesh of his flesh'. For Maximus it is sin that sets one person against another, thereby introducing division into humanity. The vices that arise through the various sinful distortions of *to thûmikon*, the 'irascible' or 'incensive' aspect of our created being, are especially prominent in this respect: hatred, slander, envy and resentfulness. But it is not only these that divide. Greed, covetousness, pride and vainglory are also well able to divide one individual from another – just as they are able to divide nations.

In all of this human ignorance plays a huge part. Maximus uses the Platonic term *gnômê*, 'opinion', to designate the state of human understanding after the Fall, and links it directly with our capacity for self-determination. It is possible for people to hold a variety of opinions on the same subject, each differing from the other: this is what we would expect in free creatures. In Maximus, however, the term takes on a more substantial meaning than it ever had in Plato or in the Greek philosophical tradition in general. He uses it more in the sense of 'disposition', a steady inclination to act in a certain way. A person's *gnômê*, therefore, is something that can change, though only slowly and with effort.

Renewing our relationship to the world

True knowledge, knowledge of the world as Christ knows it, the 'mind of Christ', is only available through the conformity of our human *gnômê* – and the intentionality, that accompanies it – with the deep structure, the *logos*, of our nature as given by God. This is the case because our *logos physeôs* is always held in harmony with the whole of creation through the divine *Logos*, the second person of the Trinity, 'by whom all things were made'.

Our fallen *gnômê*, however, with its strong admixture of ignorance, leads us into revolt against God and against others, destroying our inner harmony and thereby separating us from our own true nature that we share with all mankind. Conversely, when the human will is in harmony with its own *logos* – and therefore with the *Logos* of God – it is also in harmony with the deep structure of all human beings. Not that this automatically provides us with an easy and tranquil life. The *gnômê* of the saint is highly unlikely to be in harmony with the *gnômê* of the generality of mankind and his or her behaviour will therefore not be in harmony with their behaviour, their *tropos hyparxeôs*. To be a saint is to be out of tune with the tenor of this fallen world, to 'walk to the sound of a different drum'.

What we see, then, is that in the theological synthesis of St Maximus, the pursuit of the virtues leads quite naturally to a life in harmony not only with others, but also to a life in harmony with the whole of creation, simply because it is also life in harmony with the *logos*, the deep structure, of one's being, which is in turn an integral part of the God-given structure, the *Logos*, of the whole of creation.

Where does that leave us in relation to human activity – the whole of human culture in its extraordinary diversity – and especially, in the present context, in relation to human economic activity, which is the area that impinges most directly upon the current ecological crisis?

We have been created free, a *hypostatic* reality, just as the persons of the Trinity are hypostatic realities. The implication of this is that we have been invited – have been *called* – to continue the work of God in creation – not in the sense of a slavish imitation, not by doing only what God has already done. We are invited to be creative, but in harmony with what has been freely given us in creation. It is as if God took creation to a certain point, and then handed it over: 'The rest of the task is yours,' he says, 'but don't forget your Creator.' 'To the extent that you remember me and return to me my love while at the same time sharing my love with your fellow human beings, what you do will be good. It will fit in and develop – in ways that I have provided for but have never carried out – that original creation that I gave into your hands in the beginning.'

Maximus built his thought on the foundations laid by the Church Fathers who preceded him, modifying them in the light of the insights given him by his own experience and reflection. These foundations were in turn laid down in the course of an extended dialogue between the earlier Christian community and the society and culture into which it was born. The dialogue between the Church and the surrounding culture did not really come to an end until the Ancient World itself came to an end in Byzantium and in the West. The Fathers of the Church were well aware of the intellectual and spiritual currents of their day. Many of them were at the forefront of contemporary intellectual life. As a result they incorporated into their thought – to the extent that this was consistent with the Tradition of the Church and the Apostolic faith – the fruits of almost a thousand years of previous philosophical and spiritual reflection.

Their deepest intuition was perhaps the realisation that for the Incarnation to take place, the created world had to be of such a nature as to welcome the presence of the Son: and if, by nature, the created world welcomes the Son, then by nature it will also welcome those who conform themselves to the Son through the virtues. It will be a home for them. Those who lead a Christ-like life will inevitably find themselves making decisions that are related to the deepest purposes of God for the world, no matter in what field they happen to be working. The reason for this can be seen in the way that Maximus has related virtuous behaviour to ontology. The virtuous life is actually more 'real' than its antithesis, which is a life led in revolt against God and in opposition to one's own true nature. One must actually *work* in order to sin, for the natural state of all creatures is conformity with the deep will of their Creator. Perhaps this is why sin is so repetitive, while the life of the spirit is always new. God is simply more inventive than we are.

In the mental world of those who guide the activities of the 'developed' world in general, what we can perceive through the senses is what is real, and the most penetrating analysis of what we can perceive is provided by the mathematical insight into its functioning offered by the physical sciences. The result of this objectifying view of nature is to eliminate the beholder, that is, ourselves, from the picture of the world we carry in us. The understanding of the Fathers, on the other hand, enables us to integrate human activity into our view of what is real, and thereby secure an ontological foundation for a life in accordance with the will of the Creator, a style of life, therefore, which will not lead inexorably to the destruction of creation, but to its transfiguration, its divinisation through the divinisation of humankind. An ecologically sound life-style becomes a life-style in accordance with God's will for the whole of creation.

At the same time the whole of our inner, spiritual life becomes not just a 'return to the Father'. It becomes a return to life in harmony with the deep structure of creation as well. We see here the ecological aspect of the virtues, the 'ecology of the virtues', whereby a life lived according to God, in imitation of God in Christ, is also a life that will preserve the integrity of the created world. The detail we shall have to work out ourselves, probably with tears. It can only be worked out properly, however, in relation to the spiritual life. Thus a framework is provided for all of life, and all aspects of human life are brought into a single integrated whole.

17

Early Christians and Culture

We can see from the Gospels that in appealing to their immediate neighbours, the Jews of Palestine, the first Christians stressed the immediacy of the coming of the Kingdom. Christ's resurrection was a step on mankind's path towards the imminent end of this world. The Messiah, now known to be both Jesus and 'the Lord', would return shortly to bring justice, God's justice, to the world. Evil would be rooted out and the saints would live with God for ever. The Christian faith clearly implies a judgement of God on contemporary Jewish and (by extension) pagan society. As we can see from the New Testament, Jesus was involved in extensive conflict with the various parties that existed within contemporary Judaism. He distances himself from them quite systematically and says, in effect, 'Your ways are not God's ways.' But his message is couched in terms of an eschatological stance that accepts the language of Jewish apocalyptic and draws on the people's experience of the crushing burden of their own history, the occupation of their ancestral land first by the Persians, then by the Greeks and then by Rome, and the connivance of their own people with the forces of occupation. There is a deep sense that only God will be able to put things right and bring an end to their misery. In the meantime, Christ says: change your lives and live in anticipation of the end of time.

As we follow the Gospel, however, out into the world of Hellenistic Judaism and Greco-Roman culture (a process already described in Acts and clearly reflected in the letters of St Paul), there is a change of emphasis. Gradually the focus on the imminence of Christ's Second Coming is reduced. It remains as a deeply ingrained expectation, but does not have the same force it had in Jerusalem. The critical stance towards the surrounding world remains, but the criticism is more and more frequently expressed in terms of behaviour: the Greco-Roman world behaves in this way, but God wishes you, as followers of Christ, to behave in *this* way.

At the same time we see St Paul beginning to make use of Greek culture, both literary and philosophical, to explain to his non-Palestinian audience what he means. The result is fascinating. In order to understand St Paul we need to become familiar not only with Jewish radical apocalyptic and experiential mysticism and with what would later become Rabbinic Judaism, but also with the more familiar world of Greco-Roman civilisation. Truly here was someone who was willing to become 'all things for all men' in order to save some.

This process, whereby the Christian message is reformulated in terms of the expectations of the people to whom the Gospel is being conveyed, continued throughout the early centuries of the life of the Church. Some early Christian texts are obviously written only for those 'within', for the existing members of the Christian community. These include the *Didache,* with its description of how a local Christian community should live, and the *Epistles* of St Ignatius of Antioch. It is difficult to see what a non-Christian would make of these texts. Similarly, the *First Epistle* of Clement of Rome (*c*.96 AD) deals with matters concerning the Church in Corinth and is clearly not intended for outside consumption.[1] Much the same can be said about *The Shepherd of Hermas* (*c*.130–150), which is really understandable only in terms of esoteric Jewish apocalyptic thought, though at times it does seem to point towards a wider audience within the Church. We see here the innermost life of the Church gradually being opened up to a wider public.

The thrust of the *Epistle of Barnabas* (*c*.130 AD), however, is quite different.[2] Though it still belongs to a very Jewish world, close to the traditions of the Temple, the letter itself is written in Greek, and outside Palestine, and seems to intended not just for those who have joined the new Jewish sect, the Church, but also to other Jews who might be interested in the specifically Christian interpretation of the Temple traditions, interpretations which belong themselves to the 'Alexandrian' form of the Jewish tradition best represented by Philo.

As we move further on in time, we come upon a different group of Christian writers, generally called the 'Apologists', whose audience is quite clearly the non-Christian world in the midst of which they live. They overlap chronologically with the Apostolic Fathers, but are writing specifically for the non-Christian world. The first indication we have of such activity is the 'apology', or 'defence' of Christianity which, according to Eusebius, was written by a certain Quadratus to the emperor Hadrian, probably in the late twenties of the second century.[3] Only a short fragment of this work is still extant.

By far the most important of the Apologists, however, was Justin Martyr (100–165), also called Justin the Philosopher. He tells us (*Dialogue* 2–8) that in his search for truth he started first with the school of the Stoics; afterwards he became an Aristotelian, or Peripatetic, but then went on to become a Pythagorean. These schools did not satisfy him, and he began to follow the teachings of what we would call 'Middle Platonism'. While still a member of this school he happened to meet an 'old man' on the beach, who convinced him that what he sought in Platonism was to be found in Christ and Christianity. 'Straightway,' he says, 'a flame was kindled in my soul; and a love of the prophets, and of those men who are friends of Christ, possessed me. ... For this reason I became a philosopher, and I could wish that all men were of the same mind as myself, not to turn from the doctrines of the Saviour' (*Dialogue* 8). Justin came to Christianity at the end of a long search that involved his becoming familiar with all the main spiritual currents of his day. He found in the end that Christ alone satisfied the longings of his heart – and of his mind, his intellect.

For our purposes, however, the most important thing about Justin Martyr is the fact that he believes that secular thought has a place in God's plan for the Church and therefore for the salvation of mankind. In pagan religious thought and in pagan philosophy there is a kernel of divine truth that has been covered over and obscured by distortions that Justin attributes to the evil spirits – in other words, to the fallen state of our world. The demons have imitated and aped the truths contained in the prophecies of the Old Testament in their pagan rites. Philosophers like Plato actually borrowed from the Old Testament without revealing their sources.

This explains the similarity of their thought with the authentic Jewish traditions. On the basis of Justin's view of human history, we should not be surprised to find Christian ideas in Platonism.

In his *Dialogue with Trypho*, the earliest extant defence of Christianity against the criticism of nascent Rabbinic Judaism, Justin relies almost entirely on the Old Testament, that is, on texts that the two communities held in common, though in their Greek translation. His basic assumption is that elements of Christian truth existed before the coming of Christ, and that we should therefore expect to find it in the ancient Jewish scriptures and in any later, derivative sources. Christian truth is thus a meta-historical reality that is discovered over time. To say that it is discovered might seem to imply that it is Man alone who is involved in the process of discovery, but for Justin there are two paths through which truth comes to be known. The one is through the inbuilt ability of human beings to apprehend the truth, an ability that has been distorted by the activity of the demons, while the other is the revelation offered to us by God, as evidenced in the Old Testament scriptures and in Christ.

In the Old Testament Justin gives pride of place to the various theophanies of the pre-existent Word. The Father is beyond all description and all knowledge, but the Word can bridge the gap between God and man. As Justin says of the meeting of God and Moses on Mount Sinai:

> How then could he [the Father] talk to anyone, or be seen by anyone, or appear on the smallest portion of the earth, when the people at Sinai were not able to look even on the glory of him who was sent from him [i.e. the *Logos* or Word]' (*Dialogue* 127).

The Word or *Logos* of God is not, however, confined to

the revelation of the Old Testament – or of the New. For Justin every human being has within them a 'seed' of the *Logos* enabling them to apprehend the truth. This *Logos* of God is reflected in the 'deep structure' of the world. It cannot be apprehended by the senses, but only by the intellect or *nous*, which sees in its own way what cannot be seen by the senses – but it can be spoken about once it has been seen. This is why even the pagan philosophers were able to speak Christian truths. Thinkers such as Heraclitus, Socrates, Plato and certain Stoic philosophers can even be called Christians, since they tried to live according to the *Logos* of God, though some would think of them as atheists. For Justin, in fact, it is not just the Greeks who partake of the *Logos*, but every race of mankind.

Thus there can be no conflict between Christianity and philosophy when the latter is properly understood:

> Whatever all men have uttered aright is the property of us Christians. … For all writers through the implanted seed of the *Logos* which was engrafted in them were able to see the truth darkly, for the seed and imitation of a thing which is given according to the capacity of him who receives it is one thing, and quite a different one is the thing itself of which the communication and the imitation are received according to the grace from God (*Apology* 2, 13).

Even in the case of pagan philosophers, what they receive is given them by the grace of God. They were unable to receive it all, however, for the fullness of truth is found only in Christ, 'For whatever either lawgivers or philosophers uttered well,' he says, 'they elaborated by finding and contemplating some part of the *Logos*. But since they did not know the entire *Logos*, which is Christ, they often contradicted themselves.'

Justin goes on to link Christ and the pagan past even more closely when he says:

> And those who by human birth were more ancient than Christ, when they tried to consider and prove things by reason [i.e. by the *logos*], were brought before tribunals as impious persons and busy-bodies. And Socrates, who was more zealous in this direction than all of them, was accused of the very same crimes as we ourselves. For they said that he was introducing a new divinity and did not consider those to be gods whom the state recognised' (*Apology* 2, 10).

Justin sees human history as a whole. The issues facing Athens in the fourth century BC were the same as those facing Rome and its citizens in the second century AD. The coming of Christ does not interrupt the flow of history, nor is the search for truth essentially different now from what it was in the past. It is just that we are much better off, having been shown the fullness of truth through the Incarnation. 'Christ was partially known,' Justin says, 'even by Socrates' (*ibid.*).

The general thrust of Justin's thought on the relationship between secular, pagan knowledge and Christian truth is continued in the Fathers that follow after him. The most important of these is probably Clement of Alexandria. After Clement there was no way back: Christian thought had taken on the Greco-Roman world and its philosophy, and turned the latter into its servant. Clement had a thorough Hellenistic education and set out to prove that 'faith and philosophy, the Gospel and secular learning, are not enemies, but belong together' (Quasten, II, 7). For Clement, 'secular learning serves theology' and 'Christianity is the crown and glory of all the truths that are found in the various philosophical doctrines' (*ibid.*).

It is important to remember, however, that for Clement, faith is prior to philosophy – and indeed to science and all systematic knowledge. Philosophy will never attract anyone who does not *believe* that the world we face is comprehensible, nor will science, in both its ancient and modern forms, attract anyone who does not *believe* that the universe is structured according to universal laws. Clement understands knowledge (*gnôsis*) from the top down. The higher, which is the primary intuition given by faith, is rendered explicit by philosophy and by the Greco-Roman subdivisions of philosophy such as astronomy, music and mathematics. Clement insists that:

> The Hellenic philosophy does not, by its approach, make the truth more powerful; but by rendering powerless the assault of sophistry against it, and frustrating the treacherous plots laid against the truth, is said to be the proper fence and wall of the vineyard (*Stromata* I, 20, 100).

The role of philosophy is thus the defence of truth, not its discovery, for truth in its fullness comes to us in another way.

Thus far all these people have been converts to Christianity from paganism or Judaism. Origen (*c.*185–*c.*254), however, was born into a Christian home in Alexandria, the eldest son of a large family. His father, no doubt a prosperous man well able to give his son a fine education, died as a martyr in the persecution of Septimius Severus (202 AD) and the young Origen had to be prevented from rushing after his father to join him. All this may explain why Origen is so confident in his exposition of Christianity. There is almost no 'apology' in the modern sense of the word to be found in his writings. Christianity is simply the greater truth, able to embrace all other truths that are found in contemporary Greco-Roman culture.

The School of Alexandria, as organised by Origen, introduced its students to the full course of Hellenistic academic studies: dialectics, physics, mathematics, geometry, and astronomy, as well as to philosophy. But these subjects were just the preliminaries. In the end, Origen himself personally taught the students theology and introduced them to the study of scripture. 'I beseech you,' he says in a letter to Saint Gregory the Wonderworker, 'to draw from Greek philosophy such things as are capable of being encyclic or preparatory studies to Christianity, and from geometry and astronomy such things as will be useful for the exposition of Holy Scriptures, in order that what the sons of the philosophers say about geometry and music and grammar and rhetoric and astronomy, that they are the handmaidens of philosophy, we may say of philosophy itself in relation to Christianity' (13, 1).

The great theologians of the fourth century — Athanasius of Alexandria, Basil the Great, Gregory of Nazianzus, Gregory of Nyssa — are all heirs of Clement and Origen in that they all see Greek philosophy as a tool for the explication of the Christian understanding of the divine *Logos*, the Word of God. Among the Fathers the most developed understanding of the *Logos* of God is probably to be found in Maximus the Confessor, who made use of the full range of Greek patristic and philosophical texts. One finds in him a synthesis of classical thought with Christianity that still has heuristic power for Christians today. In fact, it is sometimes difficult to see how, in this area, it will be possible to make an advance on him.

18

'That All Should be Saved': Healing our Relationship with Science and Culture

We can judge our present position in the light of the patristic tradition, which saw the whole of knowledge – in fact, even the possibility of knowledge – in the light of theology and faith. For the Fathers, mathematics, geometry, astronomy, physics, biology and even philosophy were all, in a sense, subdivisions of theology. They studied the created world, and in doing so gave insight into God: not direct insight, but a mediated insight, gained through an understanding of the divine *Logos* that lies at the heart of the universe. The very possibility of intelligibility is bound up with the existence of the divine *Logos* and its reflection in the *logoi* of created things. Only the human *nous* is capable of comprehending and relating to the divine *Logos* as a whole, though the *logoi* of creation would seem to be accessible at least in part to the higher apes and perhaps to other creatures as well.

We could say, following Maximus, that into the original world of difference created by God, the Fall has introduced distance and hostile, rivalistic polarity. Where there was oneness and complementarity, there is now distance, antagonism, ignorance of the other and strife. The world fell apart in human experience as soon as the first couple turned their backs on the commandment of God. There is a strange experiential aspect to Maximus' understanding: we all, as fallen creatures, experience in our lives the divisions of which he speaks and we experience them as a source of pain. It would be marvellous if we, as creatures, were one with God and that for us the inner, invisible portion of our being were at one with our outer self. It would be marvellous if God's will were done 'on earth as it is in heaven', that is, in the unseen realm of the divine *logoi*, and if this world, with its obvious beauty, were again a Paradise.

On another level, however, the ultimate goal of the Incarnation, and therefore of creation, is something even greater than the elimination of distance and the re-creation of an original unity. Christ has come in order to enable mankind to become god: not God in an ontological sense, for we will always be creatures, but god in a personal sense and at a hypostatic level through becoming one with God in Christ. The language used in the Gospel of John is very important in this respect. In his high-priestly prayer before the Crucifixion, Christ speaks again and again of his being 'in' the Father and of the Father's being 'in' him. We too, as disciples, are invited into the same relationship: 'On that day [presumably at Pentecost, when the 'other' Comforter would be sent to the Apostles] you will know that I am in my Father, and you in me, and I in you' (Jn 14:20). The relationship that Christ has with the Father is to be repeated in the relationship of the disciples with Christ. They will be 'in' Christ as Christ is 'in' them. What is more, the Father himself will be 'in' Christ's disciples. The whole of the Christian life is dependent upon our being 'in' Christ and he 'in' us: 'Those who abide *in* me, and I *in* him, bear much fruit, because apart from me you can do nothing' (Jn 15:5). Distance from Christ brings an end to our working with Christ: 'Whoever does not abide not in me is thrown away like a branch, and withers; such branches are gathered, thrown into the fire, and burned' (Jn 15:6). The whole of this passage is finally summed up at the end of John 17, when Christ prays that his disciples 'may all be one. As you, Father, are in me and I am in you, may they also may be one in us ... so that they may be one, as we are one. I in them and you in me, that they may be made completely one' (Jn 17:21ff).

What we have here is a relationship that not only transcends polarity, but would seem to transcend all difference, even the difference between the created and the uncreated. At this level the difference between the visible and invisible, between heaven and earth, between Paradise and the rest of the world – and between men and women – drops away, and the created meets the uncreated at the level of personal communion (*kôinonia*). For John this is clearly the goal of Christ's Incarnation and the end point of all creation: that we humans should be one as Christ, the Father and the Holy Spirit are one. It is this that can make of man a god: this is *theôsis*. All else that a Christian might be or do follows on from and is dependent upon this possibility.

Implications for contemporary science

We live in a world whose understanding of what is 'real' is deeply influenced by the contemporary scientific outlook. It should not escape anyone that the current popular view of science is that it begins with the collection of data concerning the material world, information that is perceived by the senses, and brings order into this data by means of the scientific method. This in turn consists of the formulation of hypotheses which attempt to organise the perceptions of our senses in terms of general laws. These hypotheses are then tested through experiment, and those that cannot be confirmed through experimentation are discarded and others put in their place. This is a method, and therefore the process has to be repeated over and over again. Throughout this process the object of our investigations is matter, known to us through the senses. The hypotheses we formulate are considered to be human constructs, the products of our own thought, and thus their relationship to the 'real' is tenuous and not at all clear.

For the Fathers, however, the human being has been created in such a way as to be able to grasp the underlying meaning and structure, or *logos*, of creation. Not just the current meaning – whether or not a certain movement means that I will be attacked by a wild animal or fall into a pit, a level of meaning that would appear to be available to many animals – but the invisible deep structure of creation, the structure *because of which* the perceptible world takes the form it does. More important, the human being is able to grasp the final cause of his existence, the reason *for which* we exist, the deepest meaning and purpose of our lives. We are able to relate our lives to our Creator, and thus to perceive the *logos* of our own existence and at the same time the divine *Logos* that binds all things into one. Nevertheless, all this is only possible through faith.

The 'Big Bang' theory is widely considered to be the best way of understanding the process by which our world came into being. This theory states that the expansion of the universe from nothing (a point with no dimensions) took place in accordance with the laws of quantum physics as we have come to understand them over the last one hundred years. Note the implication of this: the laws of physics pre-existed the coming into being of the universe. What is more, they pre-existed it as an extraordinarily complex but integrated set of rules that would seem to have no intrinsic relation to the point from which the universe grew. What was the status of these laws? In what sense did they exist? *Where* did they exist if they did exist? Is this even a meaningful question? The traditional theological under-standing would be that they existed in the *Logos* of God. And if they did not pre-exist in some sense, we are faced with the virtually impossible task of explaining how they came into existence *during* the development of a universe whose expansion they controlled.

This is not the only thing that is strange and thought-provoking about modern scientific theory. Consider what is called 'the anthropic principle'. In its 'weak' form it states that the constants entering the fundamen-tal laws of physics cannot have values significantly different from the observed ones, if Man is to exist. In its weak form, the anthropic principle (developed by Barrow and Tipler on the basis of earlier work by Carter)[1] seems now to be one of the accepted basic 'givens' of science. The implications of this are enor-mous. It means, quite simply, that the size and age of the universe, even the number of stars – billions of miles and billions of years and billions of stars – cannot be understood except in relation to the existence of mankind. In order to produce man, the universe had to be what it is. The precise details of the process whereby this came about, of course, are not yet fixed, but it does appear that the structure and evolution of the whole determines local possibilities even on the smallest scale. The coherence between the general structure and evolution of the cosmos and a local event late in its history – the appearance of mankind – is truly astonishing. The existence – and therefore destiny – of mankind is bound up with the existence of everything from sub-molecular particles to galactic super clusters. It is literally 'mind-boggling'. And this is now just an ordinary part of the contemporary scientific world view.

The 'strong' anthropic principle, which states that the universe was made initially in such as way that human beings *would* appear, differs from the 'weak' form only in that it moves from what one might call an 'inherent finalism' (the end is contained in the beginning) to the acceptance of an original intentional design. Here we leave the realm of science as such; but what is fascinating is how close these two positions are. People who accept the first are not living in a different world from those who accept the second. What separates them is their assessment of the origin of all things. For the first, no meaning can be found in creation beyond what we see to exist, while for the second group the meaning of the end – and therefore of the origin – of the universe is to be found in a Creator, a being whom we may want to call 'God'.

A further example is provided by the American scientist and philosopher, Alfred North Whitehead. In his book, *Process and Reality*, Whitehead speaks of the 'lure' that the universe seems to exhibit towards an ever-greater development or fulfilment of its inherent possibilities.[2] For Maximus, who extends the notion of the *logos physeôs* to include both the coming into being, the development and the final state of every created thing, the 'form' of the goal of creation has the same inherent power as the 'form' of its beginning and development. For Maximus the *logos* of a created being not only brings it into being, but attracts it from the end, from what we see as the future, and thus exerts a serious constraint on the way it develops its inherent possibilities. For Maximus, of course, the Son and *Logos* of God is not only the integrating end towards which all things tend. In this he simply reflects Scripture: '"I am the Alpha and the Omega, the beginning and the ending", says the Lord God, who is, and who was, and who is to come, the Almighty [*ho Pantokratôr*]' (Rev. 1:8). This idea has recently been taken up favourably by Keith Ward, Regius Professor of Divinity at the University of Oxford, in his book *God, Chance and Necessity*.[3] What we see in Ward and in Barrow and Tipler is nothing other than the rehabilitation of teleological reasoning after centuries of neglect. And this rehabilitation is taking place on the basis of the scientific advances of the past half century. We cannot today ignore the developments of science if we are to present our case as Christians in the world in which we live. The influence of science on the thought patterns of our fellow-citizens is immense.

The Christian faith is about the real world and about real people. A Christianity that can present itself strongly to the contemporary world will need to explain, in terms that can be justified in the language of science, just how it is possible for one person to be 'in' another and how it is possible to receive another person 'in' oneself. This will take the study of the evolutionary development of human beings beyond the social, beyond even the cultural into the truly human – and therefore to the edge of the divine.

It is not at all clear that this can be done within the paradigm of nature that is now being used by modern science. A more sophisticated paradigm is needed, one that will include the very real acquisitions of science, but will also open out quite consciously onto the imperceptible world of the *logos*. It will need to give room to the *nous*, the faculty in human beings that is able to perceive the deep structure of reality not just in the realm of the spirit, but in the realm of nature as well. It is my belief that in order to present the case for Christianity convincingly in the modern world, we shall need to return quite consciously to the anthropology of the Fathers, to their understanding of what it means to be human, to their understanding of our capabilities and our goal – and what it is that makes it so difficult for us to move towards that goal.

What is fascinating about the world as described by Dionysius is that creation exists in three dimensions and time only at its lowest level. At all higher levels it begins to participate to a greater and greater degree in the timelessness – and therefore in non-spatiality – of God. This will be true even of the level of plant life. As a result it will probably never be possible to describe completely in mathematical terms even the nature of a plant. And if this is true of a plant, how much more will it be true of an animal – or of a human.

What is also interesting about both Dionysius' and Maximus' views of creation is that in them difference does not contradict oneness. For Dionysius this is a feature of creation at all levels of the hierarchy of existence – at least in its unfallen state – while for Maximus the integration of difference in oneness is ensured by the constant presence and activity of the *Logos* of God, the origin and goal of a process that begins with creation and ends only on the Last Day. For both of these Fathers the problem of the 'one' and the 'many' is central to their thinking. But it is central to the mission of Christ as well, though, as one might expect, Christ presents the problem in completely personal terms: how can the 'one' human race embrace the 'many' utterly distinct persons created by God? Christ's answer is that he is himself – as God and man – capable of reconciling all mankind in himself. The question and challenge he presents his disciples is whether or not they can, through him, in their several persons reconcile all mankind in *themselves*.

We know what the answer is: each human being is called to be Christ in the world, and to carry forward the work of Christ. He himself tells us this: 'The one who believes in me will also do the works that I do and, in fact, will do greater works than these, because I am going to the Father' (Jn 14:12). The fundamental work of Christ is the reconciliation of human beings and God, atonement in its broadest sense. Our work as Christians can be no more than a continuation of this work. But in order to continue it, we must be able to do it ourselves, we must ourselves be able to overcome distance, the distance that exists between individual people, the distance that exists between us and God.

This work is played out in the sacramental reality of the Church. But to defend the Tradition we must be prepared to make use of what modern science says about the real, the existent. And we should have no trouble doing so. Already the leading edge of scientific investigation points in the same direction the Tradition has taken from the beginning. But in order to make use of this opportunity we have now been given, we must appropriate not only the cosmology and anthropology of the Fathers; we must appropriate, make our own, the scientific tradition of our day as well.

This we can do this without in any way undermining our faith if we are willing to make use of the patristic doctrine of the *Logos* and the *logoi* of creation. Maximus took Christian thought in this area to unprecedented heights, but little work has been done in this area since then. It is up to us today to build upon his insights, and in doing so to integrate what we now know about the nature of the created world into our presentation of the Christian faith.

The strength of this approach lies in the way in which it enables us to understand science as a branch of theology. Human insight into the deep structure of the world, the *logoi* of nature, which is based on our ability to find meaning and form behind the confused mass of our perceptions and sensations, and then to express that meaning in language, has developed in the course of evolution in accordance with God's plan for us: that having been given freedom, we should freely choose to live like God in this world, and in this way become 'divinised', entering into the inner life of the Holy Trinity to the extent that this is possible for a creature.

Preaching to the nations

The fundamental Christian revelation is the Incarnation of the Son of God, who is also the 'Word' of God: the expression of God's personal being towards us. The Father has spoken to us through the Word not only, as Paul says, 'in these latter times', but in creation itself. The Incarnation of Christ 'in the fullness of time' cannot be separated from the creation of the universe. After all, Christ is the Lamb slain 'from the foundation of the world' (Rev 13:8), that is, from before the world came into existence.

Creation, like any work of art that extends through time, has a beginning, a middle and an end. This is true of mankind in general, and of each individual man or woman. It was as true of Christ the incarnate Son of God, as it is for all of us. For each and every member of the human race the goal is the same: that we should 'be saved and come to the knowledge of the truth' (1 Tim 2:4). Yet this is not the only expression of God's will for us in the scriptures. Again and again St John speaks of 'eternal life' as the goal of human existence. Eternal life is something that we do not have by nature. It is something that we must receive as gift, and we can only receive it from God. To receive eternal life from God is to enter into the life of God.

This may be a matter of faith, carried by the Tradition in which we live and which we accept, but our task is much more than just to live and rejoice in the Tradition and all it brings to us. We also have an obligation, laid on us by Christ, to 'go and teach all nations' (Matthew 28:19), and in order to do this we need to be able to speak a language that these 'nations' understand. How are we to proclaim our belief that we humans are able to enter into the life of God? These 'nations' to which Christ refers are not just people who live far from us, distant 'pagans' whose culture we need to study in order to know how to bring to them the 'good news' of the Gospel in the most accessible possible form. The 'nations' Christ refers to here are *ta ethnê*, the non-Jewish peoples. In one way or another they all worshipped their own, national gods, gods that reflected the state and history of the societies in which they lived. These 'nations' now surround us on every side. We live among them. They are our neighbours. Members of our own families may belong to the 'nations' of whom Christ speaks. It is they whom we must reach.

Notes

3. Meeting Jesus Christ

1. The Authorised Version uses 'abideth' here. RSV gives 'remains alone', but both this and the text of the NRSV fail to capture the implications of the Greek word '*menei*'.

2. An icon of this vision is often seen in the centre of the icon screen in a church, above the Holy Doors (which lead into the sanctuary).

3. Said by the priest or deacon as he censes the altar just before the Orthodox Liturgy begins (*The Divine Liturgy of St John Chrysostom*, Oxford: Episcopal Vicariate Publications 2008, p. 25 (see www.exarchate-uk.org).

5. Members of one body: the crisis of Baptism

1. Chrismation: anointing with a specially prepared oil, or chrism. In the Orthodox Church this normally takes place immediately after baptism (adult or infant), after which the person is admitted to communion. There is no further 'Confirmation' as in the Western Churches. When a child has been baptised and chrismated as an infant the parents are encouraged to bring him or her to communion as often as possible. At some point, the child is considered ready to begin going to Confession, after which he or she is responsible for frequency of communion, under the guidance of the spiritual father.

2. The descriptions that follow apply to the service of Baptism used throughout the Orthodox Church. The text of the service can be found in *Service Book of the Holy Orthodox-Catholic Apostolic Church* compiled and arranged by Isabel Hapgood, 6th edition (Englewood, New Jersey: Antiochian Orthodox Christian Archdiocese 1983), pp. 271–85.

3. In the Orthodox marriage service bride and groom have sponsors who hold the crowns used in the service above their heads (or place them on their heads in some traditions). In this way the

marriage is linked with the wider community, even beyond the family (there is no equivalent to the father 'giving away' the bride).

4. Most Orthodox translations of the Lord's Prayer translate the Greek words *tou ponêrou* (correctly) as 'the evil one', so that the prayer ends with 'and deliver us from the evil one'.

5. Author of *The Celestial Hierarchy* and other works of mystical theology, late fifth/ early sixth century. Cf. A. Louth, *Denys the Areopagite* (London: Geoffrey Chapman 19891). For a detailed discussion of Dionysius and his world view see Section 3.

6. Cf. Mt 28:18.

6. The Narrow Gate of Forgiveness

1. Psalm 50 according to the Septuagint numbering used by the Orthodox Church.

2. Liturgy of St John Chrysostom, which is used in the Orthodox Church except on Lenten Sundays and certain other feasts, when the Liturgy of St Basil is appointed. Quotations given here are from *The Divine Liturgy of St John Chrysostom* (Oxford: Episcopal Vicariate Publications 2008).

3. At the Great Entrance, the bread and wine to be consecrated are brought from the table of preparation in the sanctuary and carried in procession around the body of the church, before being taken to the altar.

7. The Mystery of the Church

1. Prayer before Communion, *Liturgy of St John Chrysostom* (Oxford: Episcopal Vicariate Publications 2008), p. 95.

2. Justin Martyr (*c.*100– *c.*165), *Apology* 1.46.

3. In an episcopal celebration of the Liturgy, it is normal for the bishop to stand in the centre of the nave for the opening antiphons, only moving into the sanctuary at the 'Little Entrance'.

8. The Eucharist: Radical Difference and a Common Cup

1. See 'Difficulty 41' in A. Louth, *Maximus the Confessor* (London & New York: Routledge 1996), pp. 156ff.

2. At the end of the Orthodox marriage service, the priest leads the couple and their crown-bearers in a circular procession around the lectern on which the Gospel book is placed, while hymns are sung by the choir.

3. There may in practice be two or more chalices, because of the large numbers of communicants, but theologically there is never more than one, the 'one cup' of which St Paul speaks.

9. Christian Ecumenism: a Dialogue of Difference

1. In Munich in 1982 the Commission discussed 'The Mystery of the Church and of the Eucharist in the Light of the Mystery of the Holy Trinity'. This was followed by meetings in Bari, Vienna and Freising.

2. In October of that year an Orthodox/Roman Catholic Consultation held in Brighton, Massachusetts, issued a statement referring to 'the rapid political and social changes [that] have been accompanied by serious tension which may, many fear, threaten our Churches' continued progress towards unity ... With the Joint Commission we would deplore all forms of violence, intimidation and coercion in violation of the religious liberty of persons, communities and Churches. We also encourage continued efforts by the appropriate ecclesiastical authorities to develop adequate and effective procedures for dealing with specific points of tension.'

3. The Joint Commission had met in Arricia, near Rome, in June 1991. In a working paper it said, 'the Catholic Churches and the Orthodox Churches recognize themselves as Sister Churches, co-responsible together for the maintenance of the Church of God in fidelity to the divine purpose, and this especially in what concerns unity. ... It is in this sense that the dialogue of love must be present with continually renewed intensity and perseverance. Only in this way will it be possible to overcome obstacles that seem insurmountable.'

4. Baltimore, Maryland: Johns Hopkins University Press 1986 and 1979 respectively.

5. A 'theophany' is an appearance of God to man. The Baptism of Christ is the first open revelation of the trinitarian nature of God: the voice of the Father is heard and the Spirit is seen 'in the form of a dove' descending upon the Son (Mt 3:13–17). In the Eastern Church, the Baptism of Christ – Theophany – is celebrated on 6 January, when the Western Churches celebrate the arrival of the Magi.

6. Vigil Service for Theophany in *The Festal Menaion*, tr. Mother Mary and Archimandrite Kallistos Ware (London: Faber and Faber 1977), pp. 360–84.

7. In his seventies, Maximus was declared a heretic: his tongue was cut out and his right hand cut off, and he was sent into exile, where, a few years later, he died. Twenty years after his death, the understanding he had tried to defend – that Christ had a human will as well as a divine will, and brought the two, uniquely, into total conformity – was pronounced a dogma at the Sixth Ecumenical Council (680–1), and Maximus was declared a saint.

8. The 34th Apostolic Canon is probably an attempt to sum up the consciousness of the Church at an earlier time – which is why it is called 'Apostolic'.

10. A Kingdom of Priests

1. Luke 4 – see Chapter 3, 'Meeting Jesus Christ'.
2. Cf. Mt 21:11; Lk 4:24 and 7:16; Jn 4:19 and 7:40.

11. Christ's 'Allotment'

1. *Dem. Ev.* 4.6. Eusebius of Caesarea (*c*.263–*c*.339), bishop of Caesarea in Palestine, is best known for his *Ecclesiastical History*, and other works which have earned him the title 'Father of Church History'.
2. *Hist. Eccl.* 10.4.61.
3. *Commentary on Hebrews* 1.1.
4. *The New Testament*, tr. Richmond Lattimore (New York: North Point Press 1996).
5. Fr Nikolai Afanassieff (1893–1966): an influential theologian in the original Russian emigration and professor of canon law at the St Sergius Theological Institute in Paris.
6. *Adv. Haer.* 4.8.3.
7. *Eccl. Hier.* 6.1.2.
8. *Ibid.* 2.2.4.
9. *Didascalia*: a treatise presented as being directly the teaching of the Apostles.
10. *In Leviticum, Hom.* 9.1.
11. The dialogue between priest and people that precedes the consecration of the bread and wine at the Liturgy. In response to the priest or deacon saying, 'Let us attend, that we may present the holy offering in peace,' the people reply, 'Mercy, peace: a sacrifice of praise'.
12. Cf. Acts 2:14ff.

12. A God-friendly World

1. St Athanasius (298–373), *On the Incarnation* VII 43, tr. and ed. a Religious of C.S.M.V., second revised edition (London: Mowbray 1953), p. 78.
2. Both these quotations are given in the Authorised Version. RSV and NRSV give 'life' for the Greek word *psyche* translated here as 'soul'.
3. Final verse of 'Lord, I have cried', Vespers for the Nativity, *The Festal Menaion*, tr. Mother Mary and Archimandrite Kallistos Ware (London: Faber and Faber 1977), p. 254.

13. Remembering Paradise

1. For the full text, see *The Lenten Triodion*, tr. Mother Mary and Archimandrite Kallistos Ware (London: Faber and Faber 1978), reprinted 2001, St Tikhon's Seminary Press, p. 168ff.

14. Our Place in the Cosmos

1. *Liturgy of St John Chrysostom* (Oxford: Episcopal Vicariate Publications 2008), p. 73.
2. The word 'noumenal' is used here to refer to objects of intuition or intellect, which have no phenomenal aspects – i.e. aspects perceptible by the senses.
3. *Divine Names* 4.2.
4. *Celestial Hierarchies* XIII; See *Pseudo-Dionysius, The Complete Works*, tr. Colm Luibheid and Paul Rorem (London: SPCK 1987), Classics of Western Spirituality series, p. 183.
5. *Ibid.*, pp. 185–6.

15. Dionysius and the Scientific Enterprise

1. Something like this was attempted by David Bohm, but has not received general acceptance. Cf. Bohm, *Wholeness and the Implicate Order* (London: Routledge and Kegan Paul 1980); D. Bohm and B. J. Hiley, *The Undivided Universe* (London: Routledge 1990).

16. An 'Ecology of the Virtues': the Ecological Crisis and the Objectification of Nature

1. Cited in M. Klein, *Mathematical Thought from Ancient to Modern Times*, Vol. I (New York: Oxford University Press 1990), p. 226.
2. *Discourse on Method* cited in Klein, *ibid.*, p. 226f.
3. Cited in Klein, *ibid.*, p. 308.

4. Klein, *ibid.*, p. 307f.

17. Early Christians and culture

1. The *Didache*, the *Epistles* of St Ignatius and the *First Epistle* of Clement are all available in *Early Christian Writings: The Apostolic Fathers*, tr. M. Staniforth, revised A. Louth (London: Penguin 1987).
2. Also available in *Early Christian Writings*, as above.
3. Eusebius, *Historia Ecclesiae* 4.3.1–2.

18. 'That All Should be Saved': Healing our Relationship with Science and Culture

1. Cf. J. D. Barrow and F. J. Tipler, *The Anthropic Cosmological Principle* (Oxford: OUP 1986).
2. Alfred North Whitehead, *Process and Reality* (Gifford Lectures), ed. David Ray Griffin and Donald W. Sherburne (NY: The Free Press 1978). Cited by Keith Ward, *God, Chance and Necessity* (Oxford: Oneworld 1996), p. 80.
3. See above.